A WIFE'S PRAYER

A Testimony of *Grace and Love* that Overcame
Anger, Loneliness, and Life's Disappointments

TESA STINSON

LUCIDBOOKS

A Wife's Prayer
A Testimony of Grace and Love that Overcame Anger, Loneliness, and Life's Disappointments
Copyright © 2025 by Tesa Stinson

Published by Lucid Books in Houston, TX
www.LucidBooks.com

All rights reserved. No part of this publication may be reproduced, stored in a retrieval system, or transmitted in any form by any means, electronic, mechanical, photocopy, recording, or otherwise, without the prior permission of the publisher, except as provided for by USA copyright law.

Unless otherwise indicated, scripture quotations are taken from the (NIV) Holy Bible, New International Version®, NIV®. Copyright ©1973, 1978, 1984, 2011 by Biblica, Inc.™ Used by permission of Zondervan. All rights reserved worldwide. www.zondervan.com The "NIV" and "New International Version" are trademarks registered in the United States Patent and Trademark Office by Biblica, Inc.™

ISBN: 978-1-63296-814-2
eISBN: 978-1-63296-815-9

Special Sales: Most Lucid Books titles are available in special quantity discounts. Custom imprinting or excerpting can also be done to fit special needs. Contact Lucid Books at Info@LucidBooks.com

This book contains references to childhood trauma and pornography addiction. While these topics are handled with care and sensitivity, they are part of a broader story centered on healing, redemption, and the power of forgiveness.

To God—the One who placed this desire in my heart, who gave me the stories and words to write—for providing me with the tools and people I needed at just the right time.

To my husband, Zach. Thank you for believing in me since the day I told you I felt the calling to write a book. You have always encouraged me and never doubted me, even when I doubted myself. I could not have done this without your support. You are my best friend, and I love you so much.

To Olivia and Rylee. Being your mom is my greatest adventure. You have watched me spend time writing and telling you about this book. I know it was a hard thing to understand without seeing it. Thank you for being the most wonderful daughters and for believing in me.

To my family. Mom, you taught me to love others for who they are. Your strength has always amazed me, and I credit my strength to your example of a strong woman. NeeNee, while you are in heaven singing with the angels, I think about you every time I sit down and drink hot tea and write. Nana, thank you for planting seeds that would one day be watered and lead me to Christ. Kade and Katelyn, thank you for praying with me and for me, and for loving our children. Dale, thank you for loving me as your own. Tracy, I couldn't have made it through our days at the hospital without you. You cared for me as your own and have since. Thank you for the sacrifice you made to care for me and Zach. Terry, you have welcomed me into your family since the first time I met you. Thank you for loving me as your own from day one and for checking in. I love you.

To my friends Maria, Mindy, Ann Marie, and Emily. I love each one of you. You have cheered me on since the beginning. You believed in me, prayed for me, and encouraged me. You are the iron that sharpens iron, and I am so blessed by each of your friendships. Thank you!

TABLE OF CONTENTS

Before You Begin — vii

Introduction — 1

Chapter One: God Is Faithful — 5

Chapter Two: Love Has Boundaries — 13

Chapter Three: Growing in the Lonely Places — 19

Chapter Four: We Don't Have to Do This on Our Own — 27

Chapter Five: We Are Never Alone — 35

Chapter Six: Parental Guidance — 47

Chapter Seven: Hunting for More — 53

Chapter Eight: God Works in Big Ways — 65

Chapter Nine: Finding Peace with Submission — 73

Chapter Ten: Jesus Hears Our Prayers and Sees Our Tears — 81

Chapter Eleven: Joy Comes from Our Savior, Freedom Comes from Forgiveness — 89

Chapter Twelve: Confess Your Sin — 97

Chapter Thirteen: Dropping the Extra Weight — 103

Chapter Fourteen: Finding Me and Finding Purpose — 109

Chapter Fifteen: Purpose Behind the Pain — 115

Chapter Sixteen: The Battle Is Already Won — 121

BEFORE YOU BEGIN

I have had this book in my heart for years. I have prayed for each of you holding it that you would receive specifically what the Lord has for you. Many times I have avoided writing as I was too afraid to be vulnerable. Other times I felt motivated by the Holy Spirit to write for hours. Ultimately, writing this came down to being obedient and knowing that this book was meant for you, that my story was not mine, and that it was and is God's to share.

I pray that this book brings glory to the Lord and is exactly what you need in the exact time you need it.

INTRODUCTION

People often compliment me on my positive personality, my happy marriage, and my full-life personality. What others fail to see right away when they are watching my Instagram or seeing my husband and I engage in public is that my life today is the fruit of many years of continual pruning. My husband, Zach, and I have a great marriage, but let's not confuse that with perfect. We are still growing and learning how to live together forever. After all, forever is a long time, and I guess it would be boring to get it all together right away. Life is a journey, and I started "forever" at the early age of 17.

My marriage is strong today as a result of many growing pains. Zach and I have spent time disgustingly in love with one another and times just disgusted with one another. I would even dare to say that there were times we were filled with hate for one another. Of course, no one wants to share the nitty-gritty. It isn't pretty and doesn't sit well with the highlight reels.

We are called to love Christ and love like Christ (John 13:34). We are called to love, honor, and forgive one another (Rom. 12:10,

Eph. 4:32), but sometimes we struggle with just liking each other. If we are called to be kind and loving to strangers, it should be effortless to do that with our spouse, our children, and our friends, right? But sometimes the ones we are closest to are the ones we have the hardest time showing love to.

You probably know as well as I do that the worst part of struggling is how lonely it can be. It is not easy to expose yourself to friends and family. It's hard to tell someone you are not doing well and dread going home. It's hard to ask for advice or help and explain something is not quite right at home anymore. I have attended events where I had to put on a show and pretend I was happy. The worst part of pretending is that it makes us more conscious of just how unhappy we are. It's difficult, lonely, and exhausting.

As if the stress at home wasn't enough, I began to worry what others would think. I worried that people would notice the lack of communication or public affection between the two of us and figure us out. I worried about how long we could keep our secrets safe and avoid judgment from others. I dreamed of what it would be like if we could walk through life and share our struggles free of judgment. I imagined the freedom we would have, the help we would have, and the accountability we would have if we could just share that we were in pain and needed and longed for help. I imagined the possibility of being able to receive help and offer help to others who were hurting like I was.

I longed to live in a world where we could encourage one another. I dreamed of what it would look like to not have such a high standard to live up to or, worse, fall from. I longed for a place where we know we are *all* broken in different ways. Maybe

INTRODUCTION

our hearts would hurt for one another, maybe we would be more inclined to help rather than hurt one another, and maybe showing grace would be a little bit easier. The standard from which we might fall wouldn't be so high.

Being honest could allow us to be the humble Christians God has called us to be, knowing we are all flawed and broken. We would be there to help each other through these journeys as brothers and sisters in Christ. I hope you have friends like that. I hope there are people in your corner who genuinely want the absolute best for you. People who want you to succeed because they love you. People you can be honest and vulnerable with. People you can feel safe with. People who lead you toward Christ when you lose your focus because we all turn our gaze now and then.

Our experiences are not just another story to tell. They become resources for others so we can comfort them in the same way Christ comforted us (2 Cor. 1:4). We all have stories of hurts, disappointments, and pain. My hope is that by sharing my story of how I came to the end of me and let Christ be the One who guides me will encourage you to do the same. It was not until I let go of my life and the circumstances around me that God was able to get a grip on me and change my life. So before we begin, let's invite our Father God to come along on this journey with us.

> *Heavenly Father, You have called each of us to be here at this very time. Your time is so perfect, never too early and never too late. Each person You have led to this book is searching for You in some unique way. They are calling out to You, looking for Your miracles.*

A WIFE'S PRAYER

Father God, I ask that You touch each one of them with Your healing hands, that You would move the mountains that stand so tall and intimidating before them. Lord, I ask that each person holding this book would be bold for You, stand on Your Word, and trust that their prayers are being heard. Father God, we know that all things are possible through You. Lord, I ask that You reveal Your Word to the readers of this book, that each person reading it would walk away with a renewed faith and hope in You. I pray for blessings over their marriages, their children, their families, and their friendships. I ask that You bless our time together throughout this book and that Your words would carry them through the troubles they are facing and bring them hope. You remind us in Your Word that You are bigger and greater than any fear we have. In Your loving, protecting, and healing name we pray, Amen.

Chapter One

GOD IS FAITHFUL

Make-believe is an art within the imagination. We can dream up the impossible. Our imagination is our only limit. I had a wonderful imagination as a young girl. Playing house was one of my favorite playtime pastimes. I had it all mapped out—what I wanted for a career, when I thought I would get married, how many children I wanted. It all seemed so simple, and I could not wait to grow up and one day actually have this life I was pretending.

In the meantime, I gathered supplies from the basement playroom and created a classroom for the teacher I was dreaming to be. I stacked plastic bins chest-high with a flat lid on top and pretended it was my projector. I taught all my stuffed animal students about language arts and avoided math, my least favorite subject. I was Mrs. So-and-So, happy to take the last name of my crush of the week.

I did not grow up and become a teacher. Instead, I went to college and got a bachelor's degree in social work. I don't know if you have pictured how your life would turn out, but I imagine your reality hasn't always gone according to what you fantasized as a child. I never accounted for tragedy, loss, pain, and real-life stuff of a broken and sinful world. Have you ever stopped and thought, "It wasn't supposed to be like this"?

We find ourselves in situations we never dreamed of—divorce, death, affairs, infertility, depression, unmarried when we thought we would be married by now—and the list goes on. It was supposed to be simpler than this, or so we thought. We find ourselves at a crossroads and the what-ifs of life becoming the what-is. Pain and heartache loom in our homes, and we don't know how we arrived there. We certainly don't know how we will ever get back to the way it was. Be glad when I tell you that it won't go back to the way it was and rejoice because it can be better than it was. We live in a broken and sinful world. As humans, we get caught up in the desires of the flesh (Gal. 5:17–21), and in doing so, we hurt ourselves and the ones around us.

We tend to grow and nurture our problems when we are constantly thinking and worrying about them. Are we praying about our problems as much as we are talking about them or complaining about them? Are we taking our problems to our friends and family before we are taking them to the One who can change any and every circumstance? Are we putting our worries in the forefront rather than in our prayers? We need to be taking our problems to the cross and laying them down, not to be picked up again. But that's a struggle, too, isn't it? Are we allowing our problems to lay there long enough? We say we trust in God, know He hears our cries, and know He cares about the details in our lives, but our grip is so tight on our problems that

God can't get His hands on them. We stand in the way of God working on the things we have prayed about. When 20 minutes go by or 20 days or maybe two years, we pick our problems back up and decide that God didn't answer us. Essentially, we are saying, "I trust you, but really I don't."

I know I am guilty of this. I have endured my own struggles just as you have. In 2010, I almost lost my husband in Afghanistan to an IED (improvised explosive device) blast. After two years spent living together at a hospital, recovering from the blast, I almost lost my marriage to selfish lifestyles and choices. I spent time angry at God, angry at my husband, and angry at myself. I couldn't believe God would get us through a literal explosion, extended time in hospitals, and the tragedy we suffered just to bring us home and watch us crumble due to our own devices (Ps. 81:11–13). Yet when I look back, I realize that not only did I gain, but we gained. Everything was restored to us and in better condition than it was before. That is what God does. He turns ashes into beauty.

Isaiah 61:2–3 tells us that there is comfort for all who mourn, that the Lord provides for those who grieve, that He will bestow on them a crown of beauty rather than ashes, and that joy comes in mourning. Surely things were knocked down in our lives, but they had to be for the calling that, unbeknownst to us, was on our lives.

Pain and suffering are unavoidable on this side of eternity. We all come with our own stories of tears, heartbreak, disappointments, and loss. I, too, have my share of pain and suffering even beyond my husband's injuries. After yet another disappointment, I sat on my front porch, trying to separate the hurt caused by my husband's actions from the love and faithfulness I knew were true of God. I sat there looking at my bloomed hydrangea tree. As it does each summer, the leaves were huge and a deep healthy green, and the blooms were full and white. It was beautiful, unlike my current circumstances. I stared at it and tried to think of a worship song, something to keep praise on my lips. I was heartbroken and found it hard to find joy, and then Psalm 34:1–4 came to my mind.

> *I will extol the LORD at all times;*
> *his praise will always be on my lips.*
> *I will glory in the LORD;*
> *let the afflicted hear and rejoice.*
> *Glorify the LORD with me;*
> *let us exalt his name together.*
> *I sought the LORD, and he answered me;*
> *he delivered me from all my fears.*

I knew God was near, but I was struggling to turn my face toward Him. I knew He was aware of my pain and my troubles, but I was having a hard time finding the joy I normally carry around effortlessly. Any upbeat worship song would do if I could just think of one. Colton Dixon's "Build a Boat" came to mind. I started saying the lyrics, trying to pick up enough pace to turn words into song. After all, I know God is faithful. I know what I was going through didn't catch God off guard. I knew He would, as He always had, be faithful to me, and I needed to be faithful to Him. But the same song I cheerfully sang before seemed foreign now. I couldn't pick up the beat, and I didn't want to sing.

In that moment, my own words I had once poured into a friend came flooding back to me. The same God I had preached to her was the same God who would hold me through this too. God doesn't change. His truth is everlasting, and in all circumstances, He is always faithful. I knew that. I trusted Him, but it still hurt.

My experience with my own suffering had led me to give encouraging words to my friend in her suffering. They were words of Scripture and truth. As I sat there in the sun with the heat of the morning on my shoulders, I knew those words of truth that I spoke to her applied to me too. I would rise up yet again, and my tears would not be in vain. My hurts, disappointments, sufferings, and journey would be with purpose. I would bring glory to God through this. I would be faithful to a faithful God, and I would trust in His promises. I would use my experiences and lessons learned to bring hope to others who feel hopeless.

A few years earlier, our pastor used a metaphor of a hurricane to show us the difference between how we see our troubles and how God might see them. He said that when we are in the middle of one of life's messes, all we can see is the storm around us, just like if we were in a hurricane. The wind and rain that come with the storm are hard to see through, and it becomes difficult to see sunny skies ahead. But God can see our struggles, much like the way we look at radar. He sees where the storm is but sees beyond that. He can see the clear skies all around the storm, knowing that sunny days are in our future and that there is clarity outside the storm. I love this analogy. It has stuck with me. It gives me comfort when I am in uncomfortable situations or when things seem so overwhelming that I don't know how I am going to get through them. I find comfort in knowing that even though I cannot see the clear skies, they will return. I know God sees them, and I trust that His hand is at work in my life.

First Peter 5:7–10 says we can cast our anxieties on God because He cares for us. And it says we should be watchful.

> *Cast all your anxiety on him because he cares for you. Be alert and of sober mind. Your enemy the devil prowls around like a roaring lion looking for someone to devour. Resist him, standing firm in the faith, because you know that the family of believers throughout the world are undergoing the same kind of sufferings. And the God of grace, who called you to his eternal glory in Christ, after you have suffered a little while, will himself restore you and make you strong, firm and steadfast.*

You are not alone. As Christians, we are all facing trials of this world—schemes to divide our families and cause chaos and division among our friends. Our families are our most precious thing, and marriage is a representation of Christ and His church, so what a perfect union to attack. I get it. These circumstances are not easy, but I find that in these valleys, we meet God in a way we have never met Him before. How reassuring it is to know that the power that dwells within me and my family is so threatening to the enemy that he feels the need to scheme against us, divide us to make us less powerful, or exert any energy on us at all.

When we become united, we have a force so great that the enemy finds it threatening and necessary to attack. We have the highest authority living within us, a power the enemy cannot prevail against. Knowing that gives me the motivation to fight against my enemy through prayer and claim not only my life but the lives of my kids, husband, and friends for Jesus. It should motivate you to do the same.

One of my groundbreaking moments was when I was able to look at my husband and realize our problems were bigger than him. In my anger, I was focusing on him and the choices he had made. From my perspective, he was messing up everything we had built together, and day by day, I felt more and more anger toward him. When I finally saw him as a man trapped in sin, I knew I had to start fighting the right enemy with the right tools. Ephesians 6:12 tells us that we are to put on the full armor of God because our fight "is not against flesh and blood, but against the rulers, against the authorities, against the powers of this dark world and against the spiritual forces of evil in the heavenly realms."

I knew God did not want us to be speaking to one another in the ways we were. I knew God would not want us to hurt one another in the ways we were, and I knew God would not want a division between us or a divorce. I also knew all those things were exactly what the enemy needed. Once I realized that, it was clear that I was not capable of fighting this battle alone, and my tactics needed to change.

As simple as that sounds, realizing it was a spiritual battle didn't mean Zach realized it. I had to fight differently now. I knew Zach was not who I was actually fighting, but Zach still believed this fight was a fight in the flesh. The only thing I could do was release my grip on Zach and pray for our marriage.

Chapter Two

LOVE HAS BOUNDARIES

I'd like to think I had a good childhood. Things weren't storybook perfect, but I was cared for and loved, and most of the time I felt secure. My parents had broken up before I was born, which means I never knew what it was like for all three of us to live together and then be broken up. There were many times that I craved for my parents to get back together, but I would eventually see that things were best the way they were. Eventually, both of my parents had more kids, giving me siblings to love and argue with.

My mother did all the nitty gritty raising of me. She was there for the ins and outs of daily living, school, boyfriends, homework, sports, and everything in between. She provided me with boundaries and an example of what a strong, independent woman looked like. There is no doubt in my mind that her example of womanhood is where I get my independence, confidence, and strength. It's probably where I get some of my stubbornness too. From nurturing me and my brother to mowing the yard or figuring out how to get something fixed around the house, my mom took care of everything.

Money was always tight, but we never went without anything. I even had name brand clothing to wear to school. Of course, they came from the clearance racks. That never bothered me. I was happy to be shopping at the same stores as my friends. I am sure my mom hid a lot of our hardships. I was a child, and it was none of my business. Whatever my mother did, she did a good job of it. My brother and I both went on to higher education, got married, had kids, and made something of our lives. Generational chains were broken, and the credit goes to her, all her hard work, and her devotion to us.

My dad had three more children. Four siblings is a lot, but it never felt like that. Back and forth from parent's houses, I was always aware that I was a half sibling. I knew there were parts of their lives I did not understand, and there were parts of my life they did not understand. I desired to be part of a "set." I wanted to feel fully connected to a sibling, but it always felt like there was something missing. That created a deep desire within me to one day have my very own set of kids.

I was not there when my parents split up. I don't know the entire story, and as their child, I don't think I wanted to know it all. One thing I am sure of is that life was better with them separated. They lived their lives polar opposites of each other. Mom's house came with rules, expectations, and punishment for breaking the rules. She wanted us to be kind to others, make something of ourselves, and get good grades. She did not tolerate disrespect. As any teenager would say, I thought she was strict, but I grew to respect this life. I knew the boundaries she set for us were out of love, and that made me feel safe.

My dad's house was boundary-free. We kids were a bit feral. Rules were few, and I certainly could get away with a lot under his care. As a child, I loved this. I played outside constantly, explored often, and came home for food and sleep. It was freeing and fun, but I also knew there were many times when my dad didn't know where I was. It would have been very easy for me to become involved in things that could have had lifelong consequences.

My dad and stepmom always had people over on the weekends when I was at their house. As the day continued into the evening, the smell of marijuana would creep into the vents of my bedroom. I'd just open the window and air it out. I never knew what the adults were doing, but I knew by the end of the night that they were all in rare form. In the morning, I wandered around looking for my dad and stepmom, sometimes just to make sure they were near and other times because the babies were awake and needed care.

I was about 16 when it became very clear to me that my mother was not strict. She had boundaries for us because she loved us and wanted us to succeed. That's hard to see from the eyes of a child. Hillary Morgan Ferrer gives the perfect example of the importance of boundaries in her book *Mama Bear Apologetics*. Using fire as the example, she explains that fire with boundaries is a great tool for keeping us warm, heating meals, or providing us with light. Fire, though, can be extremely dangerous when it is without boundaries. Fire without boundaries "can destroy everyone and everything you love in the blink of an eye." The firefighter and the arsonist both love fire, but the firefighter prefers it contained within boundaries.

At the age of 16, I decided it was in my best interest to separate from my dad. I had been exposed to drugs, drunkenness, and many people who made me feel uncomfortable. Yet somehow, I was protected through it all. How did a God I did not know protect me with such grace? As an adult, I've learned that there was more going on in that house than what I was aware of. My eyes and ears had been protected, and the ignorance I had was a blessing. In fact, my perception was even protected. As I write this, it sounds worse than my memory allows me to recall. Thanks be to such a good Father.

For a teenager who did not know God, I still knew that the things people said to me in that house were not truth. I knew the harsh words were not truth and that they came from a place of anger. I knew the things said to me or about me or my mother were not personal to me but came from a personal place within them. I saw my dad only four days a month, but in that short amount of time it became apparent to me that this was not what I wanted for my life. By the time I was 17, I knew it was time to place my own boundaries on my life to protect myself. The hardest part about that decision had nothing to do with me. I knew that leaving was my best choice. Leaving also meant I would leave behind two brothers and a sister. I would be letting them down. I would be saving myself over saving them. I had a way out. I could live with my mom, but my brothers had nowhere else to go. If I stayed, I wouldn't be able to save myself from more trauma. I needed to get out and not look back.

LOVE HAS BOUNDARIES

If my memory serves me right, no one made me feel bad about my choice, and no one tried to stop me. Most importantly, I made the decision on my own. God bless my mother. I knew she felt a certain way about my father, but she never expressed that in front of me. If I wanted to see him more or less, I knew I was allowed. I think that is one of the most honorable things I can think of. Even after telling her everything I had been exposed to, never once do I recall her talking badly about him to me. She had to send her daughter to a house that felt unsafe, and she had zero control of what would happen to me there.

My mom never tried to keep me from my dad. I would cry and tell her that he made me feel unloved and not good enough, and she would simply tell me to accept him for who he was. She assured me that I was loved and that I was good enough. She gave me support and space to work through those painful moments. We did not live our lives for Christ, but it's easy to see the parallel between my good mother and the good Father. I had seen a life with and without boundaries, and I had the free will to choose which life I would live. I chose love and boundaries.

I had been taught that God existed and that He was who we prayed to, if we prayed. We didn't pray often, and we went to church even less. I had gone to church many weekends that I stayed with my dad. We would gather at my Nana and Poppy's house and walk over to church. By the age of 10, that stopped. My grandmother on my mom's side supposedly took me to church here and there, but I can only remember going once. Nevertheless, seeds had been planted throughout my childhood. The soil just didn't get watered a lot, especially after I was 10.

A WIFE'S PRAYER

What I mostly remember about Jesus from my childhood was the portrait of Him—*Christ in Gethsemane*—above my grandmother's couch in her home. Unknown to me at the time, it is a painting of Christ after the Last Supper and before He was betrayed. He's on his knees facing a boulder with his arms resting on it, hands clasped together. He has shoulder-length brown hair, he is wearing a white tunic, and his face is tilted up, facing a yellow glow in the night sky.

I didn't know that Jesus prayed. That seemed odd to me. Who would the One we pray to be praying to? There was something in the portrait that touched my soul as a young girl, and thinking about it still brings comfort to that inner child. She needed to know more about this man.

Chapter Three

GROWING IN THE LONELY PLACES

There is nothing better than that wild, passionate love that makes a person crazy in all the most exciting ways. That's exactly what Zach and I had when we were 17 years old. In my junior year of high school, I fell hard for Zach, who is now my husband. He was tall and had tan skin and deep brown eyes I could get lost in. He had an athletic build and resembled more of a man than a boy.

It was January 2007, and school was out to celebrate Martin Luther King Jr. Day. Zach took me on our first proper date to the movies that day. The movie turned out to be awful, but the date I will forever remember. We had the benefit of meeting in high school, which means we could get the scoop on each other before we even met each other. From what I gathered, Zach hadn't had any long-term or serious relationships. That was okay with me. I figured we would date until he was bored, and then we would both move on. I often joke with him that he was just supposed to entertain me through the remainder of winter.

I'm not sure anyone really knows who they are as an individual at the age of 17, let alone what they want in a spouse. Our attraction was based solely on teenage hormones and physical appearances. Beginning our relationship at such a young age meant that we grew up together as we learned who we wanted to be as individuals and as a couple. We grew in our faith and struggled through some trauma, and let's throw in two children. We had two choices—grow apart or grow together. But growth was inevitable.

Growth came with a lot of growing pains along the way, years spent unevenly yoked, arguments, and new values being adopted into our lives. And let's face it, the Marine Corps and being so young added to the stress. A handful of years were spent in turmoil between the two of us, and we began to weigh if the struggles were worth it. Those moments did not seem to promise any good in our future, but we had to go through the things we did to prepare us for God's calling in our lives. Growth came out of the arguing, silence, anger, and bitterness. We learned that there were things worth fighting for, but not all things had to be a fight. Better yet, we learned how to fight in a way that solved issues and could even be respectful. God's favor was over the two of us, our children, and our relationship. Our success was not just important to us; it was important to God.

Strong marriages are tested over time. They face joys and sorrows, the highs and the lows, life and loss. We don't think about those things when we are focused on getting married. It's through these trials that we persevere (James 1:2–3). We learn how to properly communicate with one another, how we can best love our spouse, and hopefully how we can lift each other up and not put each other down when we are hurting. Marriage is supposed to honor God and be an earthly example of Christ and His church. Is that the image we are giving?

    For years, our marriage did not honor God or one another. We spent a handful of years being divided in various ways. In the first year of our marriage, we were physically divided. I lived on the East Coast to go to college, and Zach was stationed on the West Coast with the Marine Corps. The long distance was a breeding ground for arguing and jealousy. I struggled with feeling left behind and feeling jealous that Zach was living his best life while I was stuck in our hometown missing out.

    After my first semester in college, I decided I couldn't take it anymore and would move to the West Coast to be with Zach. This came as a surprise to him, and he would eventually persuade me that without a plan, it was a bad idea. He suggested a thought-out plan where we would have time to find a place to live, but that meant waiting for his next assignment. Five months after we were married, we were finally able to live together. We were headed to Camp Lejeune, North Carolina.

    We spent every day enjoying each other, and most days we went to the beach. It was fun, and most importantly, it was free. Our time in North Carolina proved to be a huge time of growth. As we look back, we refer to it as *living on love*. That's all we could afford. But this honeymoon of living together would come to an end three months after moving to North Carolina. Zach had orders to deploy to Afghanistan. I would soon be alone in North Carolina. It seemed that being together was constantly interrupted by boot camp, duty stations, training, and deployments. Now that we finally were together *forever*, we would have little if any contact for the next seven months.

Zach deployed in July, and there I was yet again left behind, this time to make a home out of a house and turn a strange town into a place I could call familiar. My heart broke, and I was constantly reminded that I was emotionally and physically the most alone I had ever been in my life.

I didn't think there was any way I could feel more alone. But I was wrong. One week after Zach deployed, I learned that I was pregnant. I was so excited, but the reality was that I didn't know when I was going to hear from Zach. I didn't share this news with anyone until I could talk to Zach. Doctor's appointments, nursery painting, and shopping—I did them all alone. I had no idea what I was doing, and I had to make all the decisions by myself.

I don't know if anyone is ever ready to have their first baby. I truly believe that is why God gives us nine months to prepare. Finding out I was pregnant with Olivia was a blessing I had no idea I needed. My days slowly became filled with more joy and less sorrow as I prepared to welcome a baby into our lives. It was lonely going to doctor's appointments by myself, but I guess the good news about being a military spouse is that you're never the only spouse doing things alone. I was surrounded with other women who were doing the exact same things as I was. I found my military spouse family and realized that being alone wasn't so lonely anymore.

Four months into Zach's deployment, I had found my rhythm. Time wasn't going as slowly as it had when Zach first left. I was growing into adulthood and trying to grow into motherhood. I had made a house into a home all by myself. I had a job and friends, and the joy of being over halfway through the deployment was beginning to set in. Only three more months of this deployment and I would see Zach again. Everything was looking up. Zach would be home, and we would have about one month before we welcomed Olivia into the world. My heart was more than ready.

As life would have it, I lost all that joy one morning with a phone call. The caller introduced himself as a staff Sergeant (SSgt), then informed me that Zach had stepped on an IED while on foot patrol. My mind stopped. I imagined my husband's body scattered in the Afghanistan dirt. The IED had claimed both his legs above the knees. His fingers had been amputated. He had internal injuries, a colostomy bag, and gas burns on his arms. His pelvis was smashed. My world came to a screeching halt. I wanted nothing more in that moment than to hear from him. Now I knew real loneliness. I sat on my kitchen floor and cried. It set in how far away my family and friends were. There was no one here with me, but even if they were, it wouldn't have been enough.

As time stood still, I imagined every war scene I had ever watched. I imagined bombs, gunshots, broken bodies, and screaming. I envisioned Zach's broken body lying in his own blood and covered in dirt as he begged for his life. I hoped someone was by his side fighting for his life when he couldn't do it himself. In that moment, I realized what love was. I had grown from that hormone-fueled teenager who focused on herself to a woman who was learning to love others above herself. Love means wanting the best for others, even if you can't give it to them. Love is making yourself less and putting others above yourself. It was clear to me at that moment that this was the first time I had ever felt this kind of love.

Stillness surrounded me. The world became slow and silent. Every thought became clearer than I had ever experienced. Every color and shape were more defined. I felt outside the world as I sat there on the floor. I became more aware that everyone else's lives were continuing.

Marine headquarters must have called my in-laws, too, because before I knew it, my father-in-law, Terry, called to make sure I was okay. The tone in his voice carried worry. I could feel the helplessness as he spoke of his son, but his voice told me he was worried about me too.

When I got off the phone with him, I did what any child would do. I called my mom. I needed my mom, and being the great mom she is, she knew exactly what to do. I don't remember telling her what I needed or asking anything of her, but I didn't need to. Before I knew it, she and my brother were on their way to North Carolina.

Zach traveled from one hospital to the next, each flight requiring him to be stable enough to make it through the flight. He finally made it from two Afghanistan hospitals to Landstuhl, Germany. I received updates from headquarters and a few gracious calls from his nurses. I longed to hear from Zach. Did he know what had happened? Was he awake here and there or just completely unconscious? I asked his nurse if it would be possible for me to talk to him. From the other side of the world, she began to explain to me that he wouldn't respond. He was in a coma, sedated.

The nurse said she could put the phone next to his ear. She warned me that he may not hear me, but I could try. I waited for a second, took a breath, and held back my tears. Just breathe I thought. I needed to sound strong and sure of my words. My throat burned and stiffened as I swallowed my tears and began to speak. "Hey, babe! It's me. I know you can't respond, and that's okay. I know you are there. Headquarters called and told me what happened. Everything is going to be okay. I just want you to know I am going back home to Pennsylvania for a day or two until you get here. When you arrive, I'll be there waiting for you in Bethesda, Maryland, where you will arrive. I love you, and I'll see you soon."

Unsure if he had heard me, I needed that conversation even if it was more of a comfort to me. I waited, but there was no response. Then the nurse came back on. I thanked her for what she had done for us, and we hung up. I lay there paralyzed in my bed, numb to my reality, and cried.

Those days were raw, etched in my memory forever. I was 20 years old and pregnant, and now my new husband was severely injured on the other side of the world. I had no idea that I was living the days that would shape me for the rest of my life. I was growing and learning things that would allow me to comfort others in need with the same comfort Christ (unbeknownst to me) was comforting me with (2 Cor. 1:4).

Each minute and each day became more and more exhausting. I finally reached the end of keeping it together. In a moment of weakness and frustration, I looked up at the ceiling through my tears and cried out, "I just need to know this is going to be okay!" I was begging anyone to hear my cries and comfort me, and it seemed useless. I hadn't directed those words to anyone, but my soul cried out, and someone heard me. In that same moment, Olivia leaped in my womb for the first time. For a young woman who had never felt that before, I knew two things in an instant. First, I knew I was feeling my baby for the first time. Second, I knew with all my being it was the subtle response from God to let me know that everything would be okay—an answer to a prayer I hadn't even prayed. Someone was listening, and He used my sweet baby to remind me that there was still life and hope.

Not once had I gone to Jesus since all this began. I hadn't prayed, and I certainly hadn't looked to Him for answers or comfort. But God found me and showed me that His grace is sufficient and powerful in my weakness (2 Cor. 12:9). He had it all in His hands. He held me in His hands, and He held Zach in His hands. I wasn't sure how, but I knew everything was going to be all right.

Luke 15 shares Jesus's parables of the lost sheep, the lost coin, and the lost son. Jesus never forsakes us. He always seeks after His lost children and welcomes them home with open arms. He is a loving Father who rejoices when we turn back to Him. He forgives us for our wandering ways. He tells us that we are always with Him and offers us everything He has. We were lost, but now we are found. We were once dead, but now we are alive through Christ.

I am always amazed how God works ahead of us. That is hard to wrap our minds around, but it is what makes His movements so profound. It's that moment when we know this couldn't have been orchestrated by humans. It's when there is no other possible way to describe a coincidence except that it was a miracle. This setback in our life was no exception. We couldn't see it then, but God had big plans for us.

Chapter Four

WE DON'T HAVE TO DO THIS ON OUR OWN

The three of us—my mom, brother, and me—packed up the first place I had ever made my own and prepared to drive back to Pennsylvania. Headquarters continued to call multiple times a day with updates on Zach. He is going into surgery. He came out of surgery. More of his leg was taken. More of his fingers were taken. I quickly became aware of just how young I was and just how much I didn't know.

I was fully responsible for medical decisions over someone's life. All approvals for surgeries, equipment being used, and medication being administered had to be approved by 20-year-old me. I was still learning how to take care of me and an unborn baby. All of a sudden, that seemed like child's play.

I arrived in Pennsylvania, and the plan was to connect with Zach's parents and then head to Bethesda, Maryland, together. Zach would hopefully be arriving in Bethesda in a couple of days. At this point I asked headquarters to stop calling and updating me. With all the amputations of nerves and limbs and the daily number of surgeries, I became overwhelmed at what to expect when I saw Zach. I didn't want to know any more. I would just find out when I saw him.

The phone call finally came that Zach was stable to make it from Germany to Bethesda. It had been four months since I last saw my husband and six days since his injury. It was time for Tracy and Terry, Zach's parents, and I to go meet him. Unknowingly, Walter Reed National Naval Medical Center Bethesda would become my home for the next two years. We walked into the hospital, and Marines greeted us immediately.

The Marines walked us around, showing us various offices, and introduced us to more Marines. They briefed us on what the next few days would look like. I don't recall much of this. My mind was set on one thing—when I would see Zach. I had imagined what he looked like, and by now I was just ready to know for sure. All this talking and walking around was preventing me from sitting at the emergency room door, waiting to see an ambulance—an ambulance that wouldn't show up for a few more hours.

As evening settled in and darkness made its debut, the three of us stood in the lobby in the company of a chaplain. It was November and cold outside, but the cold was the least of our concerns. Our eyes scanned the distance for any signs that Zach was coming. I'll never forget that moment. Fifteen years have passed since that night, but the memory of it remains fresh in my mind. I can still feel the anticipation as I stood there waiting anxiously.

Scanning the darkness for any indication of movement felt like hours were passing by. Then something finally caught my eye. In the distance, red flashing lights were glowing and bouncing off the street signs. Then the sound of sirens filled the air. The red lights got brighter, and now they weren't limited to the reflective street signs. They were bouncing off the buildings and filling all the space around us. The sirens got louder until we could finally see it—the MEDEVAC (medical evacuation) was arriving. Nerves began to fill my stomach as I realized it was happening. The unknown was about to be made known, and there was no going back to the way things used to be.

The MEDEVAC was no ordinary ambulance. It was large and provided the space and equipment to carry and care for multiple patients. It was like a small, mobile hospital. As it began to slowly pull into the horseshoe driveway where we were waiting, I became aware that the number of people around us had increased. We weren't waiting alone. There were Marines, doctors, nurses, and other families who were experiencing the same anxiousness and uncertainty.

The MEDEVAC stopped right in front of the hospital's flag lobby where flags from all countries were lined up and beautifully displayed. As the MEDEVAC pulled up, we were directed to take a few steps back. In our earlier briefing, we were told that they removed the more critical patients first to get them upstairs to the ICU and connected back to lifesaving machines as soon as possible. As the MEDEVAC's doors opened, nurses rushed in. The first patient was being unloaded. I weaved my head from side to side, trying to see around all the staff. It was certainly not the homecoming I had envisioned as a Marine wife. Nurses were rolling the first gurney out of the back and lowering it to the ground. Zach was the first to come out of the MEDEVAC, right there in front of us within eyesight. There would be no more guessing, no more distance between the two of us. He was right there.

I don't know how we recognized him. He was on a shorter version of a gurney. His legs were gone from above his knees. His hands were wrapped in tan bandages that made his arms look twice as big, and they were being propped up by two large, yellow foam blocks that looked like blocks of Swiss cheese. Two metal poles, almost a foot long each, were sticking out of this pelvis to form an X, an external fixator (Ex Fix) to hold his crushed pelvis together. On the end of one pole was a small American flag. On the other was the Marine Corps flag. Zach's eyes were closed. An intubation tube was sticking out of his mouth. He had orange, iodine-stained skin. He had lost a lot of weight since I last saw him.

The pace changed. We had gone from standing and waiting with anticipation to a pace that demonstrated the urgency of the situation. As soon as Zach was unloaded, the nurses wheeled him away. If I wanted to see him, I would have to keep up with their pace. I made my way to the gurney and stood on my tiptoes as I quickly walked along his side and kissed him. He was unconscious and wore only a white sheet to cover his naked, broken body in the cold November air.

His mother, father, and I were doing a mixture of running and walking to keep up with the nurses as they wheeled him through the lobby, to the right, and down a hallway to the elevators. They filled the elevator, leaving the three of us standing there as the doors closed, taking him away from us yet again.

While we were not quite sure what floor they were taking him to, we began to push the buttons for the second elevator. We were disappointed that we had just lost sight of Zach, something we had been focused on for a week. For the past six days, all we could think about was seeing him again, and just like that, the moment we had anticipated lasted under three minutes.

I realized the chaplain was talking to us. He went with us onto the elevator and led us to a dark waiting room with table lamps that gave off an orange glow and couches and loveseats to sit on. More families began to fill the room. Each time a doctor entered the room, all eyes turned with anticipation that we were the family the doctors were looking for. We sat and waited, watching the other families leave until we were the last ones there. When the doctors finally came back, we knew they were looking for us. We could now go back and see Zach.

It took days for Zach to open his eyes. Then, our conversations consisted of him communicating with us through blinking. As the days passed, he was able to say a few words here and there. Eventually, enough time passed where he could carry on a conversation. As the weeks continued, Tracy and I began to make the hospital and hotel room our home. Since I was pregnant, I transferred all my prenatal medical care there. It felt right to invite Tracy to join me on some of my appointments.

After learning that my baby was a girl, Zach and I agreed to name her Olivia Faith. My grandmother's name was Faith, and that was non-negotiable. Olivia sounded beautiful beside it—Olivia Faith. Later, we would learn that Olivia means olive branch, which is a symbol of peace. Peace and faith were exactly what we needed during this time. With little of a relationship between Tracy and me at that point, it is no coincidence that Olivia offered peace between us. Inviting Tracy to my prenatal appointments gave me someone to experience them with, and it gave Tracy an opportunity to be part of her granddaughter's life. It gave both of us something positive to focus on.

Tracy and I were working well together. We had two choices—try to rely on ourselves and struggle or rely on one another and succeed. We chose to succeed. We needed each other. Her being there was a blessing for me, and our working together was a recipe for Zach's healing. The three of us became our own little unit. Terry had to return home to go to work, but he drove down often to visit. He called daily, and we knew that if we needed him, he would come right away.

We were living each day by the minute and caring for one another, knowing that this was our only chance of making it through each day. Zach's needs were first in both of our minds. We knew that caring for each other was a close second. There was no room for selfish desires. Jesus tells us that first we are to love Him with all our being, and second, we are to love our neighbors as we love ourselves (Matt. 22:37–39). Any differences Tracy and I had going into this were laid down immediately, and a love between us grew in its place. In the business of those early days, I did not recognize this. It was just unfolding. Later, when the storm passed and my vision was a bit clearer, I could see that God was with us the entire time. He was holding us and teaching us. He was changing my life and changing my heart.

Looking back, there is not a single time I can remember praying. I didn't have time to turn my eyes to Jesus. I was busy waiting for doctors and nurses, and for surgeries and medications to be distributed. I relied on everyone who physically surrounded me. I relied on Tracy and turned to the limits of my own strength and power to get me through every day. By the end of each day, I had made it with nothing left to give.

What I didn't realize until later was that there were many people praying for us. They were lifting up our struggles and pain to God on our behalf. They made prayer quilts, prayed over them, and then laid them on Zach. I did not understand the power of prayer. Tracy had been updating groups, friends, and churches back home, keeping them updated and requesting fervent prayer. I was frustrated with her about this. I felt like she was sharing too much information, and I wanted to keep it quiet. It wasn't anyone's business to know what we were going through.

God knew all along that we had to endure this journey to eventually find Him. He knew where we were and what we needed along the way. He knew that one day I would see that the blessings of healing, guidance, protection, strength, wisdom, and rest would be because people invited Him into a place I did not. He knew I would learn that their intercessions were important and that it would teach me the importance of interceding for others, even if they don't believe in prayer.

> *Then the King will say to those on his right, "Come, you who are blessed by my Father; take your inheritance, the kingdom prepared for you since the creation of the world. For I was hungry and you gave me something to eat, I was thirsty and you gave me something to drink, I was a stranger and you invited me in, I*

needed clothes and you clothed me, I was sick and you looked after me, I was in prison and you came to visit me." Then the righteous will answer him, "Lord, when did we see you hungry and feed you, or thirsty and give you something to drink? When did we see you a stranger and invite you in, or needing clothes and clothe you? When did we see you sick or in prison and go visit you?" The King will reply, "Truly I tell you, whatever you did for one of the least of these brothers and sisters of mine, you did for me."

—Matt. 25:34–40

Knowing that God cared and provided for us in a time when we did not seek Him brings me to awe of His goodness. We live such selfish lives all the time, always focused on what is next. We often turn to ourselves to be our own savior. But God loves us all the time. He provides for us daily, even though we are the sinners that we are. God had spared Zach's life in Afghanistan, and we still didn't make time for Him. Our heavenly Father is so gracious and patient with us. He is a loving and forgiving Father who cares so much for His children that He never leaves us, even when we turn our backs on Him. He was always right there waiting with open arms for us to come back to Him. We did not deserve that kind of love, but He gave it anyway.

Chapter Five

WE ARE NEVER ALONE

The new year came, and Zach was no longer needing acute care. But he was also not ready to be an outpatient. The war had heated up, and there were casualties daily. The hospital was being flooded with new patients. Zach would be transferred to Hunter Holmes McGuire VA Medical Center in Richmond, Virginia. He would go there in a holding period until he was ready to come back and rehabilitate. At six months pregnant, I joined Zach in the back of an ambulance for the two-hour ride to Richmond. Tracy followed in her car.

Zach became better with each passing day. It was becoming easier to care for him. I was getting closer to my due date and beginning to focus on becoming a mother. I decided that I wanted some time alone with Zach before the baby came. I felt that Zach and I would now be okay without Tracy's help. With Zach in agreement that we could do this on our own, I had to tell Tracy it was time for her to go home.

I was terrified to have that conversation. Until now, I needed Tracy, her sacrifice, and her presence, which were not only appreciated but necessary. I needed to tell her that we were ready to try this on our own, but I worried that she would be offended, which was never my intention. We had lunch together in the cafeteria when I told her, and to my surprise, she was more than understanding. In fact, she agreed and expressed that she felt the same way. She was ready to go home to her family and felt that we would be all right on our own. While this validated my feelings, part of me feared not having her there.

I will never know the extent of sacrifice that Tracy gave for us. I know she did it with a joyful heart and would do it for any of her children. I am eternally grateful for her. I know that without her, my story would have been very different. I could not have done on my own what we did together. She was essential, and I had needed her there. I had needed her daily and on some days minute by minute. I didn't have the life experience or the physical ability to do some of the things we had to do. I know that God had us there together to grow our relationship while we cared for Zach. I grew to appreciate her as Zach's mom and love her as a mother-in-law, and she grew to respect me as her son's wife and love me as a daughter-in-law.

Back home, everyone contributed and was affected in one way or another. While some sacrifices were large, some were small and simple but made large impacts. I'll never forget a phone call from a friend who asked how I was doing. No one had asked me that yet. I thought I was doing fine, but when they asked, I broke down in tears. I had been asked daily how Zach was and often how my pregnancy was. I had not been asked yet how I was doing, and when they asked, it triggered something in me that I didn't know was there. I broke down crying. I needed to be asked that. I was okay for the most part, but I just needed to be asked. I needed to know I was important too.

Zach had been the center of my focus from November to the beginning of March, but now I was beginning to shift my focus to Olivia. I was due to have her soon, and I was four hours from my family. I knew I was Zach's main caregiver, and he needed my help. But what was going to happen when I was recovering and caring for a newborn? I ran my concerns through Zach's medical team, and they all agreed that it was best to send Zach to Walter Reed in DC so we could be closer to our family. I would be able to receive the help and care I needed from them and the hospital.

God amazes me by how He meets each one of us in the perfect way that only we can receive Him. He is never too early or too late, and how He speaks to me is different from how He speaks to you. Sometimes God uses a gentle whisper to remind me or encourage me. Other times He may use convictions or people, places, and circumstances to reveal Himself to me. One thing is for sure, though, He knows me better than I know myself, and He knows how to get to my heart.

Four months had passed since Zach had been injured. We were at our third hospital, and I had now lived in two different hospitals and a Fisher House—a home away from home for military families. Nothing about my life was stable or predictable. I had only two suitcases filled with clothing and hygiene necessities. Just as I had with each previous move, I quickly adapted to a new routine at this new hospital. Each morning, I woke up and ate breakfast. Then I walked to the hospital to visit with Zach for the day. For lunch, I ordered pizza to be delivered to the lobby. Oh, how nice Grubhub or DoorDash would have been back then. Ordering food was limited to pizza, subs, and appetizers. When evening set in, I walked back to the hotel to shower, go to bed, and prepare to do it all over again the next day.

As I continued through my pregnancy, I began to have inflammation. I knew that swelling was a normal thing during pregnancy, but what I did not know was that extreme swelling to the point of not being recognizable or having unbearable pain was not normal. Easy five-minute walks to and from the hospital to visit Zach were now excruciatingly painful and a challenge for me. The sensation of needles piercing my calves brought me to tears one day. I needed to get to the hospital, so I kept walking, stopping a few times along the way to sit and bring the pain down before pushing through it again. What I did not know was that I had preeclampsia.

Accommodations for caregivers at this hospital were in the Malonge House, an average hotel on base but for caregivers only at no cost. The caregivers were much different than the caregivers at the last two hospitals. The atmosphere was less critical and more rehabilitative. Families communicated more because they were able to relax a little more. Injured service members could get themselves to and from rehabilitation so caregivers didn't spend all day in the hospital rooms. They socialized and made friends, no longer stuck in survival mode.

I was surrounded with caregivers just like me. They gathered outside or downstairs in the café to chat. Strangers quickly became second families. Behind the Malonge House was a beautiful patio that hosted nonprofits each Saturday and provided music, food, and community. I usually opted out of these gatherings, spending my time alone in my hotel room peeking out the window every so often. Part of me wanted to be included, but mostly I found no interest in going down and mingling.

During our time at the first hospital in Bethesda, my family and friends had come down one weekend to throw me a baby shower. My mom took all the gifts back home so I didn't have to take them from hospital to hospital. She visited me and Zach often, and during one of her visits, she brought all my baby shower gifts. I would be needing them soon. I was surrounded by baby-themed gift bags filled with bottles, binkies, wipes, washcloths, towels, and baby clothes still with tags on them. There was an unopened Pack 'N Play, a large box with a baby swing in it that needed to be assembled, and countless boxes of diapers. This was supposed to be a time of nesting and preparing for the most exciting chapter of our lives. Here I was all alone in a hotel room, unsure where to put this stuff and how to assemble it. I was excited to meet Olivia but reminded I had no one to share that excitement with.

A merger of hospitals was going on, and slowly services offered at Walter Reed were transferred to Bethesda. One of them was obstetrics. Olivia would be born at Bethesda, which meant I could catch the shuttle there to receive prenatal care. I had not thought about how I would get there for her birth, but what began to bother me was that Zach was probably not going to be there for it. While other service members began working on walking and healing, Zach was still bedridden. He was unable to transfer on his own, and he could only bear the pain of sitting in a wheelchair for about an hour. He was still taking pain medication around the clock, and in order to get him to Bethesda, I would need to properly check him out on a day pass. But he would need to return for his medicine.

Not knowing when I would deliver or how long my delivery would take, this was clearly going to be an issue. We brought up our concerns to Zach's nurse who brought it up with Zach's medical team in their next meeting. She assured us that she would come back with a plan that would allow him to be at his daughter's birth. With disappointment, she returned a few days later to deliver the news that more likely than not, he would miss the birth. Zach would need to be properly checked out of the hospital on a day pass, which was typically a process that took no less than three hours.

We were crushed and felt hopeless until a few days later a social worker showed up in Zach's room while I was there. She introduced herself and told us to let her know if there was anything we needed. Feeling hopeful of the opportunity, we told her our dilemma and asked if that was something she could work on. Excitedly, she said that was "too easy," and off she went. As fate would have it, she also returned with disappointing news that she couldn't help us, and the only way to get Zach out of the hospital was to go through the normal sign-out procedure. We were beginning to feel defeated and completely disappointed.

Each day, the Marine liaisons made rounds to Zach's room. The Marines assigned each injured service member a liaison who would check in daily and see how they were doing. During one of the daily visits, we told our liaison, Eric, about our current situation and what we wanted—for Zach to be at Olivia's birth.

We told him who we had already spoken to and what their answers were. He agreed that it was unacceptable and surely there was something we could do. But he would later return like the others, defeated and with the same response.

It did not make sense. While I was gone having the baby, I would not be able to care for Zach, and Zach still needed someone around the clock. He would need help transferring to use the bathroom or take a shower. He needed help getting dressed, and he would need medication throughout the day. Each person we spoke to about our dilemma left our room with excitement in their eyes as if we had asked something of them that they felt they could fix. Every one of them came back defeated as if there were some intense forces beyond the walls of our room that would suck the excitement from each of them.

Finally, Eric came up with a plan. With his determination to help us, he gave us a typed list of who to call and in what order to call them when I went into labor. He assured me that he would keep his phone on and would be on standby to help check Zach out of the hospital for me. That would allow me to make sure I got to the hospital, and I would not have to worry about Zach. Eric and Zach could meet me at the hospital. It was the best plan we could come up with, so the three of us agreed that this was our plan. We had stressed over this plan for a couple weeks and finally had a solution.

But it's funny how God works. A better plan was about to unfold before our eyes. God knew the walls that stood in our way. He knew I would be recovering and unable to care for Zach. But God was prepared to take care of everything for us.

I was in pain around the clock now. It wasn't just limited to walking. While my doctors weren't concerned, Zach's nurses were taking notice that something was not right. Each day while I visited Zach, his nurses asked me to sit down and prop up my legs. Then they brought me ice packs. Nurses at the reception desk checked in on me, and the staff back at the Malonge House asked me if I was doing okay. Other caregivers asked if I needed anything, and I assured everyone that I was doing well. I knew the end was near and thought this was how all pregnant women felt by this time in their pregnancy.

One evening as I was walking back to the Malonge House, I came upon a woman named Lisa who stopped to chat. She had a son who was being cared for at the hospital, and he was in a power wheelchair like Zach. She offered to loan us her accessible van if we wanted to go out. While this was very kind, I most likely would not take her up on the offer. I was so uncomfortable at this stage of my pregnancy, and soon I would have a baby. It was just too much to deal with. She gave me her number just in case I changed my mind.

The service members were not the only ones being cared for. There were multiple things available to caregivers to help us through this journey. One of those services was the Yellow Ribbon Fund that assisted families with a variety of things. One thing they offered to caregivers was a free massage. I took advantage of this a couple times, but I hated leaving Zach, so I didn't do it often. It bothered me to leave him and miss a doctor coming with news or even just leaving him alone knowing he was bored. I loved being in Zach's room. I loved keeping him company and knowing how he was doing. I liked knowing when he was given medicine and who had administered it. I was in pain, though, and I needed relief. I was unsure what I could do to get that. I decided to get a massage in hopes that would help. I would go in the evening, and then I wouldn't have to worry about Zach.

I looked forward to that massage. My body hurt. The pain from the swelling was unbearable. The massage was less than relaxing, but I hoped it would give me some relief. I was amazed as I walked back to the hotel that evening. I was able to walk the entire way without stopping to take a break. I was pain-free. I finally made it back to the hotel and prepared for a shower. That is when I heard a knock on the door.

I hadn't made friends who were comfortable enough to stop by unannounced. My family would have told me if they were coming to visit. It was late, so staff at the hotel wouldn't typically need anything from me. Who could it be? I grabbed my towel and peeked out the peephole. It was Zach, and he was noticeably upset. I opened the door, confused at how he could be out of his hospital room. Without words, he leaned directly into my stomach and began to cry. He was frustrated at the doctors and nurses and just tired of being in pain. He was tired of living in the hospital and unsure when he would be released, and this evening, he had just had enough.

He must have been upset because to leave the hospital, he would have endured a lot of pain to get himself from his bed and into his wheelchair. I told him to come in and helped him transfer onto the bed. I would let him rest and calm down while I showered, but then I would need to walk him back to the hospital. He agreed and fell asleep.

A WIFE'S PRAYER

After showering and organizing all my thoughts on what had just happened, I was exhausted. I, too, needed to rest. I decided to lie down for just a few minutes and gain enough energy to return my runaway husband back to the hospital. I got dressed, sat down on the side of the bed, and rolled onto my back. As soon as my head touched the pillow, I heard an internal pop. I had never experienced that before, but I knew exactly what it was. I knew that when I stood up, everything was about to change. I lay there in disbelief for what seemed like three minutes, but I am sure it was less when everything became organized in my mind, and I had a plan. Lisa! She had given me her number earlier that day and told me that if I needed anything, including her van, to call her. I stood up, and just as I thought, my water had broken. I grabbed the paper with Lisa's number and called her.

I love this story. We had spent so much energy on a plan to have Olivia, and it was completely thrown out the window and replaced with God's perfect plan. God was working in ways we could have never imagined. I had limits and plans based on my own understanding of how everything would go, and God's plan surpassed my imagination. I asked Lisa if she could meet me and Zach in the lobby and take us to Bethesda to have our baby. "Happy to help," she told us. She said to meet her downstairs in five to ten minutes. Just like that, a new plan—a better plan—had been delivered to us right when we needed it. There were no worries about how I would get to the hospital and if Zach would be there.

I hung up with Lisa and woke Zach to tell him what was going on. He began to panic, unsure about what he needed to do. I had already packed an overnight bag, so all we needed to do was go. On our way to the hospital, I called my mom and told her I was in labor and Zach was with me. It would take my mom and brother about two hours to get there. Lisa assured me that she would stay with us until my mom arrived, and she did just that as she took care of Zach and me.

These are the stories I look back on and realize that I was never alone. I made things more complicated trying to control everything. In the end, all my plans fell through, and God provided everything we needed and desired. I relied on my own abilities and knowledge, but God who is self-sufficient and able to work beyond our limitations was faithful.

> *Listen to me, you descendant of Jacob, all the remnant of the people of Israel, you whom I have upheld since your birth, and have carried you since you were born. Even to your old age and gray hairs I am he, I am he who will sustain you. I will sustain you and I will rescue you.*
> —Isa. 46:3–4

It wasn't by chance that the only night Zach ever escaped the hospital was the night I went into labor, removing all worries of how I would get him out of the hospital. It wasn't by chance that I met Lisa, exchanged numbers, and had a ride to the hospital the very same night I went into labor. Every detail was worked out perfectly and with zero effort from me. God's provision and favor were on us.

We were never alone. God was with us the entire time, and He was constantly sending people to us when we needed them.

A WIFE'S PRAYER

I know that when situations become overwhelming and out of my control, I can rest, knowing God has it. God is faithful and cares about the desires of my heart. He knows my needs and provides them. I can place my trust in Him, knowing that He sees every detail of my life. He knows what I am facing, He knows my fears and doubts, and He has me in His hands and won't let go.

Chapter Six

PARENTAL GUIDANCE

Olivia was born two weeks early, on March 24th. And just as the doctors had predicted, Zach was discharged while I was still in the hospital, shortly after Olivia's birth. We pleaded with everyone that I would need my own recovery time, but now I had to clean out his hospital room. I lay there in my own hospital bed in disbelief. I had begged for two more weeks of inpatient care for Zach so I could get back on my feet and figure out what to do. Now I was expected to check him out of the hospital, be his full-time caregiver, care for a newborn, and recover. I was angry, but nothing could be done.

My mom and brother had come down the night before to be there for the birth. My mom, God bless her, accompanied Zach to Walter Reed to clean out his room while my younger brother stayed with me. Zach was so medicated that I am not sure he knew my mom was with him. Then she called in a panic. She had lost Zach. He was fast in his power chair, and there was no way she could keep up with him on foot.

Meanwhile, back at my hospital, everyone who walked into my room congratulated my little brother, who they thought was Olivia's dad, and me. My in-laws wanted to come and visit their new granddaughter and niece. The Marines came by to see if I needed anything, I explained that Zach was out and on the loose, and it would be great if they could find him and help my mom. Olivia was crying, and I was learning to breastfeed her. I felt like everyone was depending on me, and the weight was getting too heavy.

The Marines eventually located Zach and helped my mom with both Zach and the hospital room. Zach had been gallivanting around Walter Reed where he met Miss America, who was there visiting the injured service members. To Zach's surprise, everyone was irritated and less than impressed with his celebrity sighting as he showed off the photo of him with Miss America.

As I prepared to be discharged, a new plan was quickly put in place. My mom stayed with us for a while. I needed her there. She was happy to help any way she could. I have never met anyone with a heart for serving like my mother. She was willing to do whatever needed to be done. Sometimes that was helping Zach, and other times it was helping me. Sometimes that just meant she would love on her grandbaby. It was so great having her there. She helped me ease into motherhood, and I had someone to share those joys with. The four of us spent most of our days cramped in one hotel room.

Financially, my mom was missing work and losing income, which she really couldn't afford, but she laid all that down to care for her child. I learned a lot about motherhood from her and my mother-in-law, Tracy. I saw that a mother would drop everything for her children, and there were no boundaries or barriers that could stop her. A mother's love is selfless and unconditional. It conquers everything. I often think about how much I love my own children. I would do anything for them to protect them, to keep them happy, to show them love, and to teach them lessons in life. While none of us could ever love like God does, earthly parenting is an example of how our Father loves us.

As I thought about the things my mother did for us and as I looked at Olivia, one thing became very clear to me. Olivia would never have to wonder if I loved her. She would never have to worry if I would protect her. No matter what she ever did, I would always seek her and try to have a relationship with her. Why had that seemed so difficult for my own father? I hadn't always felt safe. I felt like I had to be cool enough and ornery enough to earn his love.

Then I remembered my mother's words. Love and accept him for what he can give. Maybe he is giving you the best he can. I never believed that as a child. It never made sense to me that I knew my mom loved me and questioned if my dad did. How did she make it seem effortless? I think she was right though. My dad loved me, and I choose to believe that he was doing the best he could, given his circumstances. I think life got out of hand, and he knew I would be okay.

Years later, my dad and I would reunite. Real forgiveness would come. He owes me nothing. I don't need him to feel badly about anything. I don't need him to say he's sorry for anything. I just want him to be happy. Both of my kids have seen him, and he loves them. He is so good with them. We don't see each other often, we don't call, and we rarely text, but I really do accept our relationship for what it is. I have learned that I am loved. I am accepted. I am enough. The relationships I have here on earth aren't to validate that but to enhance it. Whatever someone is willing to give me is enough because I am loved.

I want everyone I meet to know that. You are loved already, not because your spouse, parents, kids, or anyone else loves you but because you are loved by the King of kings who holds you in His hands, who knitted you and knows you fully. Years later, I would be reminded of this as we toured Olivia's first-grade classroom. Fear had crept its ugly head into my thoughts and highlighted all the dangers of the world. I was sharing these concerns with another parent as we walked around the classroom when she told me something I will never forget. She had been worrying about the exact same things just weeks earlier, but she took her concerns to God. As she prayed, she said she heard the Holy Spirit stop her and whisper, "They are my children. Don't you think I love them more than you do?" Those words have been etched into my heart. My kids are mine, temporarily. They belong to God's Kingdom. I am simply supposed to raise them up and train them. I can't love them better than God can. God loves them perfectly and better than I ever could.

After Olivia was born and some time passed, my mom and brother returned home. Zach, Olivia, and I quickly established a routine of how to run things in such a small space. We were still living in the hotel room. I washed bottles in the bathroom sink and set up the drying rack on the dresser. Eventually, when Olivia was on solid foods, I went down to the farmer's market and bought fresh fruits and vegetables. I cooked them in a

Ziploc steam bag in the microwave and blended them in my Baby Bullet. It was a lot to work in such a small space, but it kept me humble.

When Olivia was done playing on her mat, I had to fold it and put it away quickly. Otherwise, there was no room for a wheelchair to navigate. I had to pick up toys and keep everything neat. We had the things we needed, and we were healthy. With Zach living in the hotel room with us, it felt like we were a family, and I no longer felt so alone.

The three of us continued this for five months. When the hospitals were fully merged, we moved to the Walter Reed National Military Medical Center in the fall of 2011 and began a new season of life. This was an exciting move. We were now living in two connected hotel rooms. We had a couch, a recliner, a small breakfast bar that sat two, a kitchenette, and a washer and dryer. It was exhilarating. It felt like we moved into a mansion, and even more, there was a playground out back for kids to enjoy. There was even a daycare provided to the families free of charge. We were overjoyed with the things they gave us, and we had a new appreciation for those things and our home.

I fully believe that my worst experiences in life have brought me my best and deepest lessons in loving Jesus and trusting Him with my family and my life. I know without a doubt that I have never been left alone, I am never alone, and I am loved more than broken people can love me. I love the people in my life, and I know they love me, but they will mess up and let me down, just like I will mess up and let them down. But my worth, my value, my strength, and my purpose doesn't come from a broken world or people. It doesn't come from people who have good and bad days or change their minds. It comes from a Father who never changes. You are loved, valued, and created with purpose, not because I say so or your spouse, children, or parents say so, but because God says so. Romans 8:35–39 tells us that nothing, not even troubles, famine, death, life, angels, or demons—neither powers nor heights, depths, or anything else in creation can separate us from the love of God.

Chapter Seven

HUNTING FOR MORE

Months passed, and we settled into our new routines. Zach became more independent and needed me less. I was 22 now, and since I was 17, my life had revolved around other people. I had supported Zach through boot camp, through the Marine Corps, through his injury, and now through his recovery. I also had a one-year-old daughter. I was beginning to feel like I had gotten lost in all of it. What value did I have? I was a wife, a caregiver, and a mom, but if you took Zach and Olivia away, what was left? Zach no longer needed me for his daily needs, and as much as I loved Olivia, I needed a break. I craved something of my own. I needed something that Zach was not attached to. I needed something I worked for and deserved all by myself. I wanted to go back to college.

I began attending classes part time, and it was amazing. No one knew who I was, and they certainly did not know me as Zach's wife or the wife of a wounded warrior. I was just Tesa. Everything there was mine. My grades were grades I earned, and my friends were friends I made. I could escape there. No one was counting on me for anything. I was just a student lost in the sea of a thousand other students. I was free.

I only attended one semester before Zach completed his recovery and retired from the Marine Corps. In November 2012, he officially retired, and we returned home to Pennsylvania. We had spent two full years living in hospitals and hotels, recovering from an explosion, and having a baby. We were ready to start thinking about living life again. For the past two years, life had seemed more like a pause than living. Moving home felt like freedom. It seemed to promise more possibilities, hope, and the excitement of living again.

A couple months before we moved back, we flew to Boston and met with an organization called Homes for Our Troops. We had settled on land, but our home wouldn't be complete until December the following year. Until the house was built, we settled into a townhouse. I began going to the local university to complete my bachelor's degree. Olivia was now in daycare, and Zach found a new hobby—hunting.

We moved into our home in December 2013. It was what we had waited for and dreamed of, our first home where we could fully settle in as a family. We could finally hang photos on the wall and unpack every last box. This was a permanent move that promised happiness, and we were more than ready for it. The only problem now was that all our problems we had been too busy to notice settled in with us.

Zach was living in the civilian world for the first time since being a Marine. He was no longer living in a place that catered to his medical, emotional, and physical needs, and he was no longer surrounded by people who were just like him. Men didn't look like him, and he couldn't relate to them. His disabilities and life experience left him feeling isolated.

It wasn't just Zach who felt lost. I also realized that I was no longer surrounded by other caregivers. While we had friends who were married and had young children, our daily lives looked a lot different than theirs, and that was lonely and frustrating. I was envious of wives whose husbands carried baby carriers and pushed strollers. I was angry that husbands opened car doors for their wives while I had to load my child and then my husband and finally get myself into the car. I hated that Olivia couldn't take balloons home from birthday parties since it was too stressful if they popped and sent Zach into shock. I became very aware of everything that felt stolen from me. Surely no one understood the challenges I faced.

I wanted to go to the beach, but it was difficult to push a wheelchair in the sand. I wanted to go on dates with my husband without getting dirty from lifting a wheelchair in and out of a car. I felt robbed of my youth, robbed of my marriage, and robbed of motherhood. Zach was unaware that I was struggling with these things. How could I tell him that I was angry? I wasn't angry with him, and I didn't want him to feel responsible for something that was beyond his control. I was angry that this was the hand we had been dealt, and there was no one I could admit that to.

I was surrounded by people who loved me. We lived close to Zach's family and my family. I was often with my mom and friends, and everyone checked in to see how we were doing. There was one conversation with my mom that I often reflect on. After asking me how everyone was doing and telling her we were all fine, she continued with her concerns. She empathized with my struggles, recognizing that I had a lot I was responsible for and that it was okay if I wasn't okay.

"Were doing good, Mom," I told her.

She went on, telling me that it is important to take care of myself too.

"I know. I am good though," I assured her.

She knew I was deep in caring for everyone around me, too busy to care for myself. She feared that one day it would all crash, that I would crash. She was right. It wouldn't be for another two years, but I, in fact, would crash, no longer able to bear any more weight on my shoulders.

Leading up to my breakdown was Zach's lack of participation with our family. Olivia and I began to live a separate life from Zach. We lived together, but Olivia and I would spend the day playing, riding bikes, going to parks, or being with my mom. Zach stayed home all day in bed on his iPad. I dropped off Olivia at daycare, attended classes, and then picked up Olivia. I was bitter with Zach. After all I had sacrificed for him, the least he could do was be an active husband and father.

Here I was again, begging to be loved and given attention from a man in my life, but this time it was my husband who was neglecting me. Olivia was the best part of my life. She deserved a daddy who loved her and gave her attention. Zach was completely detached from us. As he lay in our bedroom, Olivia and I went about our lives physically, emotionally, and socially detached from Zach. He certainly didn't do bedtimes, bath times, doctor's appointments, or anything else. My patience was beginning to wear thin.

I just could not live a life where I had to beg someone to love me, and I never wanted my daughter to experience that either. I was standing in the kitchen stirring spaghetti sauce when I turned around to see Olivia playing on the living room floor. Zach was lying on the couch, lost in his iPad, both unaware of the other's presence. Maybe a divorce would free us all. I would be free from this marriage, and Zach would be forced to interact with Olivia when he had her. I broke the silence with the offer.

"I'm not angry. I think we should split. It would be helpful for everyone. You would have Olivia when I wouldn't be there. I think it would help you interact with her. I just don't know what you bring to this family anymore."

I was calm and honest. Somehow it didn't even come out harsh. I wasn't angry. I was tired. I didn't want to hurt his feelings, and it seemed like the only solution to our problems. He didn't want a divorce. He apologized and said he would try to do better moving forward. I nodded my head and returned to cooking. But it was far from over. The thought of separation was something I had been thinking about, and I was already preparing to leave. I just needed to finish college first.

I could see Zach trying to be better. He made the effort to participate with Olivia and asked me what he could do to help, and then he would do it. But his efforts began to fade over time, and we were back to where we were before. I was frustrated that Zach was able to travel all over for hunting but unable to help with anything around the house. I didn't need him to move mountains but maybe just cut his own food, get his own drinks, fold some laundry, or play with his daughter.

Zach was traveling a lot now. I had no idea that at all times of the year there was hunting to be done in some part of the world. That didn't bother me. If Zach was traveling, then he was away. I loved when he was away. The house ran more smoothly without him, and it was peaceful.

What I did not know was that Zach was struggling with his capabilities and limitations. I was frustrated with a husband who seemed lazy. But he was struggling internally with how he fit into this world. Neither one of us knew how to navigate our new life, and we didn't know how to communicate that. I knew Zach was capable of more than what he was giving us, but he didn't feel capable of being a husband or a dad. I had expectations of him that he was never going to meet because he did not know what his own expectations of himself were.

When I look back on turning points in our marriage, I come back to a night that Zach had returned home from, yet again, another hunting trip. After bringing all his stuff into the house and taking a shower, he came into the kitchen where I was preparing dinner. Proudly, he began telling me all the exciting things about his trip. While the stories included the actual hunt, he also told me about the conversations and the fun back at the cabin. With excitement in his eyes, he told me that at the end of each day, the men all returned to the cabin to prepare dinner together. His face was lit with enthusiasm, and mine was lit with irritation. Why were these men so great that he was helping them?

My frustration went away as quickly as it came. I looked at his face and saw how proud he was to tell me he tried to cut his own steak and was able to do it. As a grown man, he had been too proud to ask for help on his trip. At home, he was safe with me. He could ask me for things, and I would bring them to him or do them for him. I don't know what made this trip different than the others, but something pushed him out of his comfort zone to try to help himself. He was able to get his own drinks and help prepare food, something he did not know he could do. What he returned home with was confidence and purpose. He found part of himself that he had lost. Now he had the confidence to be part of our family and the courage to see what else he was capable of. I had believed in him all along. I knew he had more to offer, but he needed to see that for himself.

Christmas 2009 I flew out to Washington state to spend Christmas with my new husband.

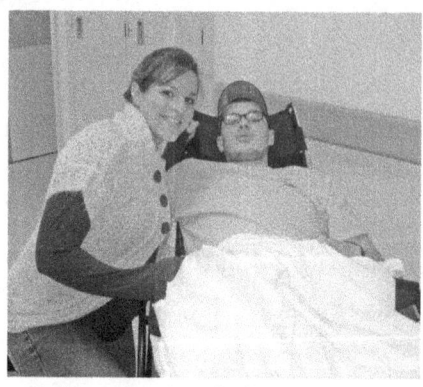
Richmond as described in chapter five

Zach leaving for deployment, July 2009. As described in chapter three.

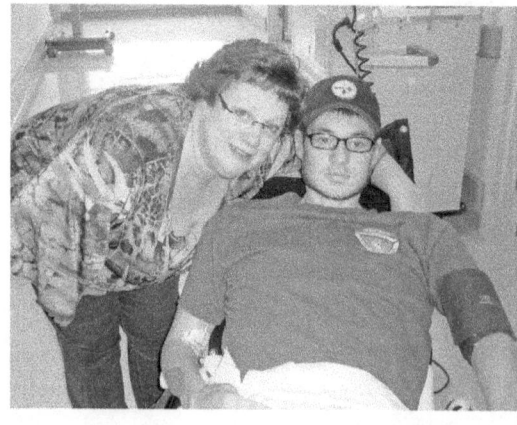
Zach and his mom, Tracy in Richmond as described in chapter five

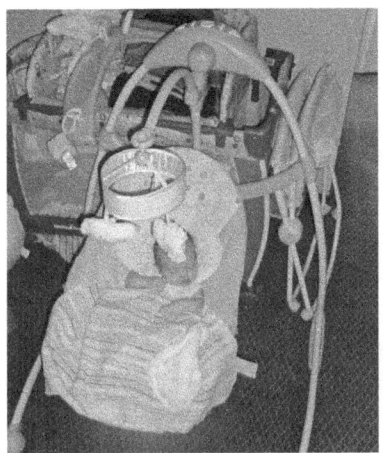

Olivia in our hotel room where we lived for the first five months of her life. Everything we used had to be returned to their place when we were done using them as described in chapter six.

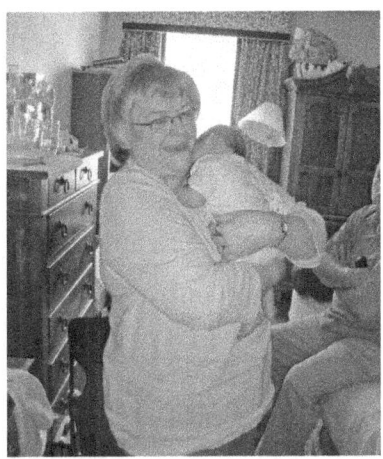

My Nana and Poppy came to meet Olivia. In chapter six, I described how we had to utilize all areas of the hotel room. Bottles were washed in the bathroom sink and dried on the dressers. Lotions and diaper bags were stored above the second dresser. As you can see in the background, there was a place for everything, and everything is in its place.

My mom came down almost every weekend if she could. She spent hours with us, helping or just visiting. This is her and Olivia take a nap in Zach's hospital room one afternoon.

Zach's dad, Terry spent a lot of time traveling back and forth from his home to the hospital any time he could. It was hard juggling work, a family, and caring for his son.

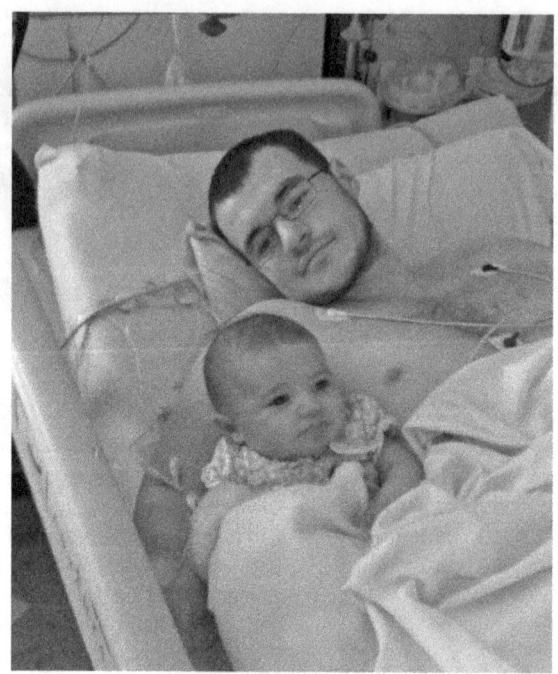
Olivia visiting her daddy at the hospital

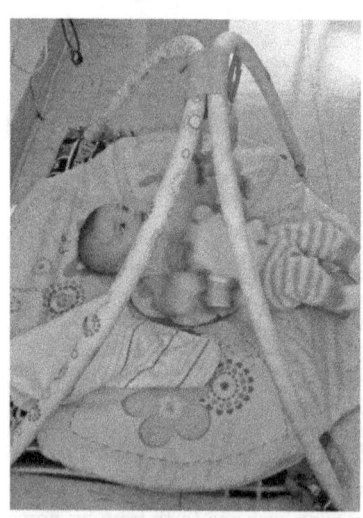
Olivia and I would walk to the hospital each morning and not return until evening. I kept toys in Zach's hospital room to occupy her during the day.

Zach and Olivia learning to walk together

Chapter thirteen, our trip to Destin Florida was life changing. I grew so much during this trip, letting a lot of things go that I could't control. Finding myself again.

In chapter thriteen I talk about the photo that I posted. My mother in law commented that we seemed changed or rested, not knowing this trip had impacted me so deeply. No one knew the growth that had happened to me during this trip.

Chapter Eight

GOD WORKS IN BIG WAYS

With a long road still ahead of us, things were starting to slowly get better. Zach was helping with small things around the house and engaging with Olivia. At three years old, Olivia was apprehensive toward Zach, which left him feeling discouraged and often unloved. It was a real-life lesson of reaping what you sow. He had not invested in a relationship the first three years of her life, and it would prove to be difficult over the next couple years as they developed one. He kept trying, and as time went on, things got better between the two of them.

In the meantime, I began to want a second child. While things were not perfect between the two of us and I still had an exit plan in motion, I wanted another baby with him. I wanted Olivia to have a full brother or sister.

With Zach's injuries and evaluations from doctors, we knew that natural conception was not possible. We would have to seek in vitro fertilization (IVF). We also had concerns that Zach had been exposed to burn pits in Afghanistan. He had returned with E. coli, Acinetobacter, and pseudomonas. Would our baby be at risk for birth defects? Would we be able to handle Zach's physical disability *and* a child with a disability? Unfortunately, there was not enough data to determine any of that. It would be a risk we would have to assume if we wanted more children. To me, it was worth the risk.

Zach and I went back and forth on this for months. He was happy with one healthy child and couldn't understand why that was not enough for me. I knew I would not be happy with one child. My heart desired to have another one. I wanted Olivia to have a friend. I needed her to have a sibling to do life with. I knew deep within me that if I only had one child, I would resent Zach for the rest of my life. Maybe I already did resent him for taking so much of my life. I felt that the least he could do for me was give me another child to love after all I had done for him. This was not negotiable for me. A second child was something I wanted, and I would have one at any cost. I had been more than understanding and flexible for the past few years. I had no other choice but to accept the things that had happened to us, but having a second child was not something I was going to allow to be stolen from me.

With much convincing on my part, we sought out nearby specialists and began to learn what the process of IVF would look like. It would be physically, emotionally, and financially exhausting. There would be labs, injections, medication, and surgery, all at a high price. None of that mattered to me. I was ready to begin anything that brought me closer to having a baby.

GOD WORKS IN BIG WAYS

We left the doctor's office and got into the car. We said nothing to one another. I was too afraid to say anything because I already knew what he would say. Breaking the silence, Zach looked over at me and simply said, "We can't spend that money." One round of IVF would cost $10,000, and multiple rounds would be $20,000. We would have to pay it out of our own pockets because in 2014, there was no insurance or financial help from the government for family planning, even though this was a service-related injury. Things have since changed, praise God.

I just sat there. I knew Zach was going to say no. I was disappointed. Again, I would have to sacrifice something I wanted. Constantly I was being reminded that life is not fair. I couldn't help but wonder why I deserved this. I had been a good person. I had stayed by Zach's side, encouraging and helping him through rehabilitation. Why was I constantly being punished? Could God not see the things I had done? Surely, I was due some sort of reward.

What I could not see then was that a blessing was coming my way. God was about to show up for me in a way that I didn't just get what I wanted. I was about to see God's hand in my life and learn who God is. I would learn that God is the God of the possible and that He can work beyond the minds and talents of humans. If we had agreed to go through IVF at the quoted price, I would not have learned that God does, in fact, give us the desires of our hearts.

We contemplated adoption and fostering but were unable to reach an agreement on anything. Finally, in frustration, Zach threw his hands in the air and simply said, "If you can figure out how to get the money, you can do it." I heard yes and needed nothing else. I would research facilities, call local government offices, and figure something out. Everything between us felt so divided. I wanted a baby. I wanted us to go to church. I wanted him to be more present in our lives and lead our family. I felt like he had no desire for any of that, and I wasn't sure how much longer I could take it. I was still going to college, and now I was trying to figure out how to afford IVF. I needed to get my degree and have a second child, and then I needed to get out of this marriage.

I began calling organizations and nonprofits to see if they could help us with IVF. I called local government agencies and officials' offices, but no one could help me. Finally, I found the A.R.T. Institute of Washington, a fertility clinic at Walter Reed. They provided fertility treatments to military families at a lower cost since they were a teaching school. I had made the drive to Walter Reed so many times that I knew I could do it again and alone if I had to.

I couldn't share with many people the struggles we were having. We were still very new in our community, and everyone knew who we were. Zach was the local hero, and everyone wanted him to speak somewhere or show up somewhere for one thing or another. We had to present ourselves as a strong unit for everyone watching.

With no one to confide in, I took my concerns to God. Even if He wasn't fixing anything in my life, I knew He saw what was going on. I told Him I wanted another baby, and I told Him I wanted to be happy. I didn't care what my life looked like as long as I was happy, and I was okay being a single mother. Then I told

God I wouldn't leave my marriage until He told me it was okay to leave. Then I waited.

I could sense the Holy Spirit telling me that I was going to have another baby. I found comfort in that feeling. I knew God was going to provide me with another child to love. I just did not know how or when. Would we go through IVF, or would we adopt or foster? The only thing I was certain of was that our family was not complete, and it would be.

I called the A.R.T. Institute and set up an appointment. As a teaching hospital, they did IVF in groups. That meant we would become part of a group or class that was going through the process on the same timeline. The next group was scheduled to begin in August. If we couldn't make that work, we would have to wait until spring. Not knowing much more, I signed us up for the program, and we drove down to attend the first meeting. In an auditorium, we sat with other families reviewing slides on a large screen and listening to each provider talk about who they were. There was only one thing I needed to know. How much would this cost?

After we received all the information on what our responsibility would be for IVF, we sat down with the financial team to discuss the price. This was where I was the most nervous. I dreaded the idea of hearing any number that would tell me this is not going to happen. I braced for the impact.

"Your total will be $3,500."

Surely, she meant for the first month of injections and medications. That couldn't include the egg retrieval, sperm retrieval, or embryo transplant. I asked what the total cost would be.

"Your full total will be $3,500. That includes everything."
"No hidden costs?" I asked.
"No," she replied.

How could this even be possible? I felt like this was too good to be true. Would we be hit with a big bill we never saw coming? We could do this. We could fully pay for IVF, and we wouldn't even need help. After months of calling people and searching online for clinics, it was all over. I felt like my prayers were finally being answered. The financial burden was just lifted off of us. I was overjoyed.

A few days later, I received a phone call from one of the nonprofits I had contacted weeks before. They apologized that they were unable to help us with family planning, but it had been weighing on their hearts, and they sent a check in the mail. She assured me that it was not much, but it was what they could do. When the check arrived a few days later, I was in complete shock. In pure perfection, as if God wrote it Himself, it was for $3,500.

I was in complete awe. I had tried to find financial help for months, and now the burden was completely lifted. I felt God right there at the end of my driveway holding that check. God is always in control. He saw the bigger picture and knew every single detail. If I would have gotten what I wanted when I wanted it, I would have missed God. Now I knew He saw all my tears, He knew my frustrations and anger, and He was there with me all along.

We went through IVF that fall and conceived 10 embryos. We successfully transferred one embryo, which resulted in a successful pregnancy. In the spring, I delivered Rylee Grace, our healthy, spunky, wild child. My prayers had been answered, and I was beginning to see how faithful our God is. Life was flowing smoothly, and I finally felt like our family was complete. That is when the A.R.T. Institute called to confirm that we had conceived and birthed a healthy baby. They asked what our plans were for the remaining embryos.

We had been so overjoyed with the pregnancy and birth of Rylee that we had completely forgotten about the nine embryos in storage. Now we had to decide what we were going to do with them. Uneducated on embryos and options, we listened to what our choices were. We had three choices: destroy them, donate them to science, or find an adopting family who would like to transfer and raise them. This was quickly a no-brainer for us. Those embryos were created with much love, prayer, and intention. They were miracles and evidence of God. They were our babies and Olivia and Rylee's siblings. Of course, they weren't born yet. They were safely stored away, but they were our babies, our children. We also knew we could not birth and raise all of them. We chose to love and parent them by giving them life and giving them a family.

Our story now intertwines with two other families. While our prayers were being answered, it was beyond our understanding that the prayers these other couples were praying were being answered at the same time. Those nine embryos were never meant for me and Zach. They were always meant for the families they were born into. Zach and I were just part of the journey. We are blessed with two open adoptions where we get to watch these children grow and connect with their parents, and our children know their siblings. We are blessed with a big God who never gives up on us, works beyond the human mind, and answers prayers in miraculous and powerful ways.

> *"For I know the plans I have for you," declares the LORD, "plans to prosper you and not to harm you, plans to give you hope and a future. Then you will call on me and come and pray to me, and I will listen to you. You will seek me and find me when you seek me with all your heart."*
>
> —Jer. 29:11–13

Chapter Nine

FINDING PEACE WITH SUBMISSION

The more I dove into learning who God was, the more I desired for Him to be part of my life. The closer I was to God, the more it felt like there was division in my marriage. That confused me. God was good, and having a relationship with Him was good, so why was getting closer to God getting me farther away from my husband?

I have learned over the years that this spiritual divide is not just something I have faced but something many of my friends have too. Unity in the home becomes difficult to establish, and it begins to feel like the more you seek Christ, the more hostile the home gets, which contradicts what you're seeking in the first place. Arguments over attending church, tithing, and hanging out with certain friends become sources of conflicts. The shows, movies, music, and how we choose to raise our children become battlegrounds. It begins to feel like following Christ is only making things worse at home. What a horrible trap that is to fall into. The lies of the enemy tell you to surrender and go back to living your life for yourself, not fighting for your family's revival.

I felt defeated and exhausted trying to keep my focus on Christ and my sanity and remain calm at home. Most days I felt like I had my back up against the wall. Zach was supposed to be the head of our family and lead us toward God, and it felt as if he was pushing us away. I wanted to attend church, but I couldn't make him. I wanted him to pray with me and our children. I needed him to help me create a home where the Holy Spirit was welcome, but at this time in his life, he just was not ready.

I had to make a choice to do these things without Zach and pray for him to one day join us. I would have to assume the responsibility of leading our family until Zach would step up to the plate. Sometimes that meant I was the one to take the kids to church or pray with them. I had to practice self-control and grace over anger. I was determined to show my children how wonderful our God is and, in the meantime, pray that God would catch Zach's attention.

Many days that left me feeling defeated. Zach had been raised in the church, so he knew better. Why was it so difficult to get him to just do the right thing? The longer this went on, the more irritated I became with God for not just making it happen. My efforts and prayers felt useless. I found myself trying to make Zach feel convicted of the things he was doing but ended up criticizing and condemning him. I was trying to help him by speeding up the process to get him to Jesus more quickly than he was getting there on his own.

FINDING PEACE WITH SUBMISSION

What I failed to realize was that I was probably pushing Zach farther away. All I was doing was bringing more stress to both of us and not trusting that God wanted Zach's heart more than I did. I wasn't trusting that God's timing and lessons would be better than my own. The more I tried to be in control of Zach, the less I was demonstrating a heart like Christ. I felt righteous and better than Zach and thought he should follow my lead because I knew what I was doing. Boy, oh boy, was I wrong!

> *Submit to one another out of reverence for Christ. Wives, submit to yourself to your husbands as you do to the Lord. For the husband is the head of the wife as Christ is the head of the church, his body, of which he is the Savior. Now as the church submits to Christ, so also wives should submit to their husbands in everything. Husbands, love your wives, just as Christ loved the church and gave himself up for her to make her holy, cleansing her by the washing with water through the word, and to present her to himself as a radiant church, without stain or wrinkle or any other blemish, but holy and blameless. In the same way, husband's ought to love their wives as their own bodies. He who loves his wife loves himself.*
> —Eph. 5:21–28

These were the verses I was reading and using against Zach. I was so caught up in how Zach was failing in my eyes that I failed to see my own faults (Matt. 7:3–5). I was so obsessed with trying to fix him that I couldn't see that I was doing the same thing. I was supposed to honor my husband and submit to his leadership. Even though he had not surrendered his life to Christ, I should have focused on loving him and showing him grace through this time and not criticizing and nitpicking everything he was doing. I should have focused on loving him and leading him to Christ through love.

God commands wives to honor and submit to their husbands. There are two roles addressed in those verses, and I was so hung up on what Zach was doing that I overlooked the command to put on my role as a wife. Zach, like me, has free will. I cannot make him pray, and I cannot force him to live his life less for himself and more for Christ. I cannot control him, and I shouldn't desire to do so. I am, however, in control of the choices I make. Am I going to honor God by honoring my husband?

I have been blessed with a husband, and I am his helper. My husband is my provider, my companion, and my partner through life. Together we should both be striving to help each other live our lives in the best way possible. When one of us is slipping, we should encourage them, extend grace, and be forgiving, gentle, and loving. We should pray for one another and serve one another above ourselves. I believe that when I do that, regardless of Zach's actions, God sees my heart and my obedience. I believe God rewards us for the things that go unseen and often unappreciated. I trust that God hears my prayers, sees my tears, and knows my heart. I trust that He will care for me.

Submission and honor have proved to be challenging for me over the years. I had suspected and known that Zach struggled with online pornography. Usually I knew it simply because the Holy Spirit burdened me with suspicion. Other times, I caught him, and even fewer times he simply confessed it. His actions certainly did not leave me feeling as though he was honoring me above himself and his own desires. Instead, I felt betrayed, disrespected, and hurt by his actions and lies. I was left feeling undesirable and not enough. As if all the internal feelings were not enough of an insult, when I asked him why, his reply was filled with harsh words as he tried to take the responsibility off of himself. He looked at me and told me that it was because of my body.

I was very much aware that I was overweight. After birthing two babies, I was even more aware that my body looked different. I struggled with that on my own, and I really didn't need anyone else affirming all my insecurities. Not only was it hard for me to look at myself, but I knew it disgusted him too. I carried that around with me for a while, and although I forgave him for saying that, I will always remember those words and how they cut.

I tried to shift my focus to Christ, digging deeper into His promises and believing He loved me no matter what. I tried to find peace in a broken body and give glory to God that my body could nurture and birth babies. No matter how imperfect my body was, it was no excuse for adultery on any level, and it certainly didn't warrant such disrespect. In that moment, which hurt terribly, I had a choice about how I would respond, so I walked to the bathroom, locked the door, and prayed.

Zach is a double amputee whose body is covered with scars and battle wounds, but I never see him as not good enough. I was in disbelief that after all the trauma he had gone through he would tear another person down for how their body looked. Rather than pick apart his body and meet him with the same hurt and hate, I chose to walk away before I, too, said something that would live with him forever, something that would live with me forever, and something I would never be able to take back. It wasn't that I accepted disrespect by not firing back; it was that I have been called to be loving and Christ-like. My responsibility to obey Christ does not rely on anyone else's words or behavior.

While unkind words in that moment would have possibly made me feel good that I had gotten even with him, I would have felt really badly that I had chosen to be so hateful. I know that his words were lies, spoken from guilt and shame from what he had done. I know the scars on my body are from giving life to our children and that my body shape and size does not define me. It took years to heal from those words and truly learn that no one can give me value except Christ. I am His, and His love is enough. Nothing can separate me from His love (Rom. 8:31–39).

I carry that lesson with me. I don't hurt from what Zach told me that day. The lesson I learned was about self-control and doing what is commanded of me, regardless of others. I wanted to get Zach back equally to how he had gotten to me, but every day after that day, I am grateful that the Holy Spirit kept me quiet. The fruit of self-control is a promise delivered. I never want to hurt anyone like that. I don't want to tear down God's children and leave them with scars that never fully heal. I want to reflect God's love, and I want to live up to the calling He has given me. That feels so much better than the guilt of hurtful words that escape our lips in a moment of hurt and anger.

We live in a world where being our own savior is encouraged and self-sufficiency is admired and respected. Our world promotes that respect is only given if it is deserved. It would be weak to serve a man and no less to serve a man who did not warrant that respect. How can a wife submit and follow the lead of a husband who is not submitting and following the Lord? That is where we have to make the choice to honor Christ by honoring our husband. That is where you continue your wifely duties, knowing that your actions are for the Lord and not for human masters. Our inheritance and reward are from the Lord Christ, the One we are actually serving (Col. 3:23–24).

You are sure to get a mix of responses when using the word *submission*. I get that. I struggled with it for a long time. I began looking at it differently when someone pointed out that submission is a form of protection. How could that be? Being vulnerable did not seem to promise protection. Submission in a marriage felt more like slavery.

The truth is that we all submit daily to something or someone. The employee submits to their boss. The child submits to their parents. The citizen submits to the law. Jesus submits to the Father. The husband submits to Christ, and the wife submits to her husband.

There is protection in each of those submissions. The employee is protected by the boss who has limits on how many hours a week the employee can work and what the paycheck will be. The child summits to the parents who have lived and known the dangers they are protecting their child from as they create rules and boundaries. The citizen submits to the laws that keep order, create standards, and protect liberties.

Jesus, the Son, submits to the Father who called Him to die a brutal death on the cross to save us from our sins (Heb. 5:7–9). In the Garden of Gethsemane, Jesus begged the Father to take away, if possible, the death that was before Him, but only if it was the Father's will.

When our husbands submit to Christ, they are seeking the Holy Spirit's wisdom and guidance to lead their family. A godly husband wants his wife and family to succeed. He wants what is best for his wife and for her to fulfill the calling on her life. As a wife, we can rest in that protection. The choices we make with our husbands who seek Christ cannot fail. If they fail by human standards, we remain in the protection and care of our husbands and our Lord.

By honoring our husbands and submitting to them, we are honoring Christ. But what if my husband is not honoring Christ? I've been there too. There was a season when I had to follow my husband's lead, knowing his decisions were based solely on his own desires. I prayed for him and our family. God knew my heart, and I asked Him to protect us as we followed Zach's guidance. I was able to find peace in knowing that my heart was right with Christ and that He would care for me, His daughter.

There are so many times I have been frustrated when meals I prepared, clothes I washed, and moments I bit my tongue instead of lashing out went unnoticed. I had to keep my faith in Christ that the things I did to serve my husband or the things I resisted from saying were seen by Christ and that He knew my heart. As I continued to seek God rather than lash out at my husband, I began to see my prayers being answered. During this season, just to make it through each day, I would ask God to help me see Zach through God's eyes and to love Zach with God's heart because my eyes and heart did not see anything worth loving or staying for.

Chapter Ten

JESUS HEARS OUR PRAYERS AND SEES OUR TEARS

It was December 2017, and Zach and I were back at one another's throats. The arguing was at an all-time high. It was daily, and it was intense. Absolutely everything he did or didn't do angered me. We deployed weapons of cursing, screaming, and name-calling. My resentment toward him was seeping out. I was constantly angry. I kept a mental list of all Zach's wrongs, ready to use them. At any point, I was prepared to justify why I had a right to be angry. I viewed him as selfish and inconsiderate of anyone except himself. The choices he continued to make hurt me, and I found it impossible to believe that they were actions of someone who loved or cared for me.

After putting the kids to bed one night, we had yet another argument. This one led to Zach telling me to "just get out." It wasn't the first time he had told me that. He used it often. Eventually, it became less of a threat and more of an invitation for me. Get out. Those were the words I was waiting to hear again. They were my ticket to get out and be free from this life. I wasted no time grabbing suitcases, clothes, and odds and ends. I pulled the girls from their beds, and the three of us went to my mom's house.

We didn't stay long, only a week before returning home. Zach had begged for me to come back home, and although I was unsure if that was what I wanted, I eventually agreed to go home. I spent the next month sleeping in the living room, not wanting to share any intimate space with Zach. I lived out of my suitcase that I hid behind the couch so the kids or unexpected guests would never see them. I spent that month debating what I wanted before I finally committed to work on our marriage. I knew that made Zach a little uneasy. He tried many times to talk to me or convince me to sleep in the bedroom, but I didn't feel like we were a couple anymore, and I wasn't sure I wanted to. I knew I had to make a decision to commit to this marriage or get out of it.

Time did not feel like it was healing these wounds. Zach and I only grew more distant and hateful toward one another. I felt as though he had ruined my life. I had given him years of my life, years spent sacrificing for the Marine Corps and caring for him while he was injured, only to spend the rest of my life living in misery. Any conversations between us only involved necessary topics such as the kids or appointments. It was tense, surface, and painful. I loved going to work and hated being at home. As a daycare teacher, I had both of my kids there with me and was surrounded by a classroom of kids who were medicine for my soul. I was appreciated for healing boo-boos, playing, and providing food. I was awarded with hugs and affirmation. Work was my escape and healing for my soul.

Unable to hide my pain from my coworkers, they all knew what was going on at home. That's when one of them shared with me the book *Fervent* by Priscilla Shirer. That book changed my life, and I highly recommend it. It taught me how to pray fervently, specifically, and intentionally. I learned how to pray for myself, my marriage, my family, and my purpose. I learned the authority I have over my life and my family. I learned that I needed to fight this battle—not against Zach but against the enemy—with Jesus, the only weapon I needed.

I had been trying to control everything. I went to work all day just to come home and take full responsibility of the house. Knowing Zach was home all day and chose not to help only fueled the fire of the bitterness I had been harboring. I took care of all the needs of our children. Due to Zach's lack of self-control with pornography, I had locks on every TV, iPad, and phone. I raced home every day trying to catch Zach watching pornography and prove that he was lying. I searched his electronic history, and all I ever found was stress and exhaustion. I had to let go of my grip on Zach. It was suffocating both of us. If I was ever going to heal, it wasn't going to be because Zach stopped watching pornography. I needed to heal from feeling robbed of my life. I had to heal from betrayal, rejection, broken trust, and the feeling of not being enough. I had felt these things as a little girl, and now I was feeling them again as a grown woman. It was all too familiar.

I knew Jesus was the only way to get the healing I needed. How could I expect the Holy Spirit to work on Zach with my hands so tightly wrapped around him and our situation? I would only be able to control me. I couldn't control the things Zach said or did. I couldn't control how he felt and what he was or wasn't doing and what I felt like he should or shouldn't be doing. Trying to control him and how I wanted him to be made me disappointed and hurt.

My lunch breaks became time to drive around aimlessly and pray. I parked in vacant parking lots and quiet developments that gave me space to read, pray, and cry. That went on for four months. While nothing was getting better at home, I was finding that talking to Jesus was giving me peace in an unpeaceful time of my life. I was finding hope, trusting that my prayers were heard and would return answered.

God was hearing my prayers and seeing my tears. I saw this all come together one afternoon on my lunch break. As I sat parked in a development, crying hysterically, I began to beg God for a breakthrough, any kind of breakthrough. I had no more left of myself to give, and I felt completely hopeless in all my efforts. I no longer cared what pain or discomfort it would take to get me to happiness. I needed God to do something now. I couldn't imagine anything hurting worse than how I had been feeling for so long. I was at the end of my rope, and I needed everything to change.

I begged. "God, please, please help me to be happy again. I am done. I have no more to give. I'll do whatever it takes to be happy again. I am ready."

Hysterically, I cried aloud to the Lord, lifting my voice in hopes He would hear. I begged for His mercy over my life. I poured everything out to Him, seeking refuge in Him. I was desperate. I needed Him to save me from this prison of a life I was living (Ps. 142).

Instantly, a sudden calmness came over me like a blanket. I stopped crying and knew right away what the Holy Spirit was telling me. *My* heart needed to change. That couldn't be right. How could it be my heart that needed to change when Zach was the one who had caused all this? It was his actions and his hurtful words. I had been so infuriated with Zach's betrayals against me that I hadn't realized my own transgressions against Christ. My heart had become hardened over the years. I had built up walls of resentment and hatred, and it was time for my heart to heal. My heart needed a makeover.

> *Get rid of all bitterness, rage and anger, brawling and slander, along with every form of malice. Be kind and compassionate to one another, forgiving each other, just as in Christ God forgave you.*
> —Eph. 4:31–32

I had to let go of Zach. He was no longer my problem. Zach was now God's problem. I sat in my car on my lunch break and changed my prayer.

"He's yours, God. I will no longer get in Your way. Forgive me for trying to control him and this entire situation. I need to feel better. I want to change. Help me, God, to see Zach through Your eyes. I know You love him. You can see the good in him when I cannot. Help my eyes to see differently. Amen."

I fully released Zach at all costs. I no longer wanted to try to fix him, and I no longer cared if we couldn't work it out anymore. I talked to Jesus every day all day. I tore pages out of the book *Fervent* and taped them and scripture to my bathroom mirror. My gaze was focused now and crystal clear. I was ready for battle with the help of God beside me. I realized we were being attacked spiritually, and my weapon of choice was prayer. I asked God to show me something each day in Zach that was worth loving. I knew God loved Zach. I just couldn't see what He saw in Zach. I felt I needed to make the choice to tell Zach each day that I loved him, even though I didn't feel it. I knew the motions would have to lead me for a while until the emotions caught up.

A few weeks went by, and things began to get even worse. Life was exhausting, and everyone was unhappy. As the two of us stood in the kitchen, I asked Zach if he was happy. I knew he wasn't, but I guess I just wanted to hear him say it. He told me that the only reason he was in this relationship was for the kids. It didn't hurt to hear that. I felt the same way. The kids were a huge driving force to continue to fight for our marriage, but even that was wearing out.

I kept reading and praying. My relationship and dependence on God was greater than it had ever been. I was on fire for Jesus. I could feel Him daily and hourly. While life around me seemed chaotic, I was at peace with a Father who loved me and cared for me. That's exactly what He did. Through prayer, I felt the Holy Spirit give me an assignment to pray over our home. Zach wasn't there at the time, and I wanted to do it before he got home. I needed to touch everything—the walls, bed, couch, kitchen, pillows, bathroom, dressers, everything. As I touched them, I prayed prayers that sounded like this: God, I pray for the couple who sleeps in the bed that they will be a happy couple in Jesus's name. I pray, God, for the family who sits on this couch and watches this TV that they will be a happy family in Jesus's name. You get the point. I touched everything I felt led to and prayed specifically for us, our family, and our happiness. When I was done, I opened my doors and yelled to the enemy, "You are done here! We have believed your lies for the last time. You are no longer welcome here. This house belongs to the Lord Jesus, and where He is, *you cannot be!*"

It was a holy anger that came over me as if the Holy Spirit took over my body and was angry at the lying schemes that had created such a mess in our lives, in our home, and in our minds. It was anger at the enemy for stealing so much ground from our family, and I would no longer tolerate it. The evil one had his last shot. He had stayed far beyond his welcome, and it was time for him to go. I was ready to reclaim my marriage. I was done allowing this misery to go on any longer. I sobbed in prayer on my knees just to stand back up and yell at that devil to get out in the name of Jesus.

I had never prayed like that before, and when I was done, I was calm and felt peace. I knew right away that when Zach returned home, I needed to welcome him into our "new home," Our cleaned-out home. Our fresh, enemy-free, God-fearing home.

So that's exactly what I did. When Zach came home, I did as the Holy Spirit had prompted. "Welcome home," I told Zach. No response. I kissed him, which was awkward and landed flat, but I took no offense. I had a renewed spirit and confidence in God. I knew things were moving. God was in control now. I had lain everything at the foot of the cross, and this time I didn't go back to pick it up.

It had been four months since we had shown any physical affection for each other, and it all began to change after this. Walls were falling, and my heart was changing. I looked over some of my journal entries, one from a church sermon called "God Allows Crisis to Give Us an Opportunity to Have Faith." I had to walk through all this to find God in such a powerful way that I would never go back. I had to grow in my faith because I needed Jesus.

Troubles still come my way, and I still have to face them, but now I never have to face them alone. My faith allows me to believe that whatever happens to me, God takes care of His children.

Chapter Eleven

JOY COMES FROM OUR SAVIOR, FREEDOM COMES FROM FORGIVENESS

At some point in our lives, we stop and ask ourselves if we are happy. Am I happy with my career? Is my marriage bringing me happiness? Am I satisfied with my parenting and my children? Am I happy with my friendships? There are so many things, places, and people who bring us happiness, but happiness comes and goes as quickly as our emotions and moods change.

I am happy in my marriage as long as everyone is contributing and getting along. I am happy with my parenting when I am complimented on my children's behavior. My job brings me happiness when I am successful or my boss gives me words of affirmation. All the people, places, and things in my life are meant to bring me happiness and add to my life in a positive way. But it is not happiness that we truly seek. What we really want is joy, and real joy is best found in something that is unshakable, something that doesn't have bad days and change its mind. Our joy has to come from God, our unshakable rock. This lesson was one I learned the hard way.

It's very easy to look at my husband as my rock. He is, after all, my provider, my best friend, and my life partner. I have expectations of him. I need and want him for a variety of things in my life. I have expectations that he will be faithful, provide me with love, help raise our children, hold me accountable to certain things, help me when I struggle, hold me when I cry, celebrate my successes, and so much more. From the time Zach and I first began dating until about a year after his injury, he provided these things effortlessly. It became easy to place him in the center of my world. From the moment I met Zach, he brought me joy I had never experienced before. I had found a man in my life who healed all wounds of rejection I had once carried with me.

That sounds quite magical, but it was problematic. I placed all my purpose and faith in a man, a human who would inevitably let me down. It's not that Zach was or is a bad person. Zach is quite an amazing man, although flawed as we all are. It was only a matter of time before I would be completely caught off guard by his actions and lose my joy and identity in the process.

Zach had been struggling with pornography during all our relationship, and while I had my suspicions, he always assured me that my suspicions were wrong. I had prayed that the Holy Spirit would expose anything hidden in darkness and reveal sin. But when I confronted Zach, he told me he respected me too much to do such a thing. I walked away feeling guilty for accusing him. I even prayed that the Holy Spirit would not allow the enemy to get into my head and make me doubt my husband. When I finally caught him in his lies and he could no longer persuade me from the truth, I fell apart in disbelief.

I had wholeheartedly believed it was impossible for Zach to hurt me. I had placed him on a throne so high that it shook everything I knew. I felt betrayed, and I began to question why I was not good enough. Why was it so hard to love only me?

I turned my hurting heart toward God who had the ability to prevent it, but He didn't. We struggled with this same topic for years. It was the same arguments and the same pain of betrayal and rejection. I know who God is. I know He can take away temptations and heal broken people and marriages. Why wouldn't He do it for us? Our marriage had suffered so much already. It didn't make sense that a loving God would allow more pain and for our marriage to crumble.

On one occasion, after yet again learning that my husband had continued to lie and hide his secret sin, I walked away rather than yelled. What point was yelling? I had done that a handful of times before in response to the same situation, just to get nowhere. After yelling and crying, I was still left with the familiar feelings of betrayal and rejection. I walked around until I found myself in the bathroom. I felt safe there. The room was small, and that felt comforting. I shut the door behind me, and as quickly as I locked the door, tears raced down my cheeks. I lowered myself to my knees, surrendering. Was it too much to ask my husband to be faithful to me, to not search outside our marriage for sexual satisfaction?

I thought we were happy. We were intimate and loving toward each other, flirting and playful. I sat in the dark on my knees on the hard bathroom tile, my head in my hands. My mind began to slow down, and I lifted my face. The glow of the moon through the blinds caught my eyes. I stared at the bright night sky through the cracks of the blinds and whispered, "How could You allow this when You know everything we have been through?" As quickly as I asked, I got an answer. In the most honest and gentle response, I felt the Holy Spirit whisper back, "Zach is sitting on My throne, and you won't remove him, so I did."

I knew right away that the Holy Spirit was right. I was relying on Zach for things I should have been looking to God for. Zach was only human and incapable of being God. And God would never lie to me, betray me, cut me with harsh words, or fail to keep a promise. Zach, friends, family, and jobs will let me down from time to time, but God will not. My joy could no longer be rooted in things that change or people who can change their minds. Zach could bring happiness to my life, but I couldn't hold him responsible for bringing me the stability of joy. What a mess that would be. What a mess that had been. My joy had to come from someone who didn't change due to a bad day or a mistake. My joy couldn't be based on the job I have, the spouse I have, the clothes I wear, the church I attend, or the friends I have. Sure, those things add to my life and bring me happiness. But my enduring joy could no longer be built on them. My joy had to come from Christ alone from that moment forward.

God has always wanted to sit on the throne of my life, but I have allowed other gods to sit there from time to time. I've allowed people to sit there only to learn that they will disappoint me and cannot maintain that position in my life. We each fight flesh versus spirit (Gal. 5:17), and we all need forgiveness when we succumb to the temptations of this world. Holding anyone responsible to never let me down or disappoint me is not only unrealistic but very unfair to hold them to such high expectations. Zach is human, and I needed to forgive him. When he committed his next offense, I found that I needed to forgive him again (Matt. 18:21–22).

Forgiveness becomes an ongoing practice, but it hasn't always been limited to my forgiving others. I've learned over the years that I also had a lot I needed to forgive myself for. I have let people down, been far too critical of others, tried controlling situations that belonged to God, and the list continues. What I have learned is that I am blessed to have a Savior who took on a brutal death for me, for all of us. He shed His innocent blood so we would be forgiven once and for all and be able to spend eternity with Him. If Jesus is willing to forgive anyone who asks for forgiveness, then I, too, can forgive those who sin against me.

I chose to forgive Zach, and over time he would make the same choices. I would choose to forgive him again and again. With each offense, I learned more about who Jesus is and how we don't deserve His forgiveness, but He is gracious and gives it freely. If He could forgive those who sinned against Him, then I had to do the same.

This battle with pornography and lying became too familiar. But overtime I found that I began to hurt not just for me but also for him. He had promised himself that he wouldn't do it again, but he couldn't resist the temptation. He had been living with a secret and a fear of being caught. Zach hadn't just been sinning against me and our marriage. He had to work this out with God. Again, I found myself changing the way I prayed. I didn't want Zach to just stop watching pornography; I wanted him healed of the addiction. I prayed that all the years stolen from our marriage, all the years of lying and secrecy would be redeemed, and God would use them to bring Him glory. I didn't just pray this; I believed it.

Choosing forgiveness and keeping Christ at my focus gifted me with freedom. Forgiving Zach gifted me with peace and comfort. Zach could still choose to go down that road. He could still choose to lie about that or something else, but I know I don't have to fight that battle alone. When I turn it over to God, the battle is already won, and I can rest. My joy will no longer be robbed by temporary circumstances.

I have now spent over half my life with my husband. Through all the mountaintops and valleys, we have learned to be best friends. I love the man he has become from the 17-year-old boy I once met. He's flawed, but he strives daily to be better. He is human and will make mistakes. As his wife, I want to be the gentle place where he can be vulnerable, where he can safely land. I want him to know that if or when he makes a mistake, I will help him. I am on his team.

> *But he gives us more grace. That is why Scripture says: "God opposes the proud but shows favor to the humble." Submit yourselves, then, to God. Resist the devil, and he will flee from you. Come near to God and he will come near to you. Wash your hands, you*

> *sinners, and purify your hearts, you double-minded. Grieve, mourn and wail. Change your laughter to mourning and your joy to gloom. Humble yourselves before the Lord, and he will lift you up. Brothers and sisters, do not slander one another. Anyone who speaks against a brother or sister or judges them speaks against the law and judges it. When you judge the law, you are not keeping it, but sitting in judgment on it. There is only one Lawgiver and Judge, the one who is able to save and destroy. But you—who are you to judge your neighbor?*
>
> —James 4:6–12

I've had to humble myself and remember that I, too, needed this same grace but maybe for different reasons. Holding Zach to such a high standard and casting my judgment on him was another sin I would have to answer for. God knows my hurts, and I had to trust that He would lift me up (James 4:10).

Chapter Twelve

CONFESS YOUR SIN

The next few years would prove to be the hardest. My marriage was tested as we took steps forward just to take a few steps backward. When I felt we were making progress, I would learn months later that it was all lies, and Zach still couldn't lay down his addictions. He would continue to lie and hide his trails. For a while, I spent time and energy trying to catch him. I checked history on the TV, the phones, and the iPad. I watched his face for muscle movements that did not match his words. I did this for a while until I realized it was not something I wanted to keep up with. I just did not want to live a life babysitting a grown man.

More important than the testing of my marriage was the testing of my faith. I knew God knew things I did not. He sees things I cannot, and I needed to trust that if there was something I needed to know, He would tell me. After all, I was the one who begged God for healing and happiness. I needed to stop picking up what I had lain down at the foot of the cross. I had to trust God over my husband. I had to trust God with my life.

I had become sensitive to TV shows, music, movies, and social media that glorified sex or women in provocative situations or poses. When scenes came on TV, I felt tense and uncomfortable, almost like a child watching something I knew I shouldn't be watching. I would glance over at Zach in hopes that he felt the same way. He never did, and that would often lead to arguments. I tried to prove why watching those scenes was wrong, and he tried to defend why they were okay.

On one occasion, we went to Target to grab a few things we needed. Of course, walking around the store, we inevitably peeked at the new movies and books. A popular medieval fantasy TV show that everyone was watching at the time was available on DVD, and Zach bought it. We were always looking for a new show, so we set out to watch the first few episodes. We were only one episode in when I no longer could take it. Sex was a common theme. It wasn't simply implied that the characters were having sex; it was graphic and constant.

I lay there while the show played. I prayed that God would talk to Zach and that he would be led to turn the show off. The show continued with marital affairs, orgies, rapes, molestations, and incest. The longer I lay there waiting for Zach to turn it off, the angrier I became that he didn't.

When the episode ended, I told Zach how I felt. He began defending his desire to continue with the series. It was a popular show, and he justified that everyone had good things to say about it. We argued, and it was clear we were not going to see eye to eye on this.

I spent the next couple of days praying over this disagreement, knowing he had continued with the series on his own. It was clear that I was not going to stop him from watching what he wanted to watch. I just wanted God to put an end to this, obviously by stopping Zach. Instead, I got a lesson on conviction. As I prayed, it became clear to me that we are not always at the same spot in our spiritual walk. I was feeling conviction over supporting a show that abused the gift of sex. My convictions were not the same as Zach's, and I was the only one responsible to make sure I was being obedient to my convictions. If there was anything convicting Zach or not, that was beyond my responsibility.

That applies to all our relationships. It is easy to judge other Christians by the things they do and say. Our convictions are going to be different because our relationship with Christ is personal.

I moved forward, trying to understand this. Just as I felt Zach would make two steps forward and three back, I am sure God felt the same about me. I trusted that God would reveal Zach's secret sins, and when I felt sure Zach was lying and God wasn't revealing his sins, I found myself searching for proof yet again. I always came up empty-handed, only for the Holy Spirit to expose it months later.

Eventually, I began to see a pattern. In all my searching devices and all my accusing Zach of lying, I never discovered anything. Instead, it was in the moments that I felt peace and felt strong enough to handle the truth that the Holy Spirit prompted me to ask Zach, and Zach would confess. My demeanor was completely different in those moments. My words were gentle, and my agenda was to be his friend and help him, not sentence him to another fight. I knew God was revealing truth to me in the moments I could handle it. It was in God's timing, not mine.

I had to change my mindset on this. I couldn't be a wife looking to catch her husband misbehaving. I had to be a friend trying to help someone I love overcome something bigger than himself. I had to separate Zach from my husband to my friend, and he needed me to be his friend through this.

We recycled this pattern for a while. He would fall into temptation and hide his sin, causing him to lie. I would suspect it, beg him to be honest, and come up empty-handed and angry. Then I would be reminded that I laid this down and needed to faithfully trust Christ. Shortly after, truth would be revealed. We were both struggling with our own temptations.

Each time we did this, I walked away with my faith stronger than the last time. My reactions started to turn from anger to disappointment that we were still doing this to eventually my heart hurting for him. I began to see Zach as a man who was captive to something bigger than himself, and that broke my heart. This was not about me not being good enough. The enemy had a hold of Zach, and as his wife, I could not allow that.

Our children were now old enough to know when something was going on between us. We didn't argue very often, so when there were tears and silence, they know something was not right.

This past summer, one of our daughter's friends had an overnight birthday party. Her mother is a close friend of mine, so I offered to stay and help. It was a great time of bonding, and let's face it, I love that my teenager doesn't mind me tagging along. We returned home the next morning, and as we came in, Zach confessed that he had slipped up. It was the first time he had ever offered this information. I was disappointed, naturally, but I quickly remembered what God said about confessing our sins. When we confess our sins, God forgives us, and the enemy no longer has a hold on us (1 John 1:9). We no longer carry shame or guilt (Ps. 32:5). Instead, we have healing (James 5:16).

This was a breakthrough. It was something to praise God for, and I also found that Zach's honesty didn't hurt nearly as badly as his lies had in the past. Healing was quicker, and trust was not broken this time. It felt like a mountain was moving.

Zach's confession didn't stop there. Our oldest daughter was worried about why her mom was upset. I didn't want to expose her dad. It wasn't my place. Instead, I told her it was adult stuff and that I couldn't share it with her. That must have been on Zach's mind because a couple days later, when it was just the three of us riding quietly in the car, Zach broke the silence.

"Olivia. Do you know why your mom has been so upset?" he asked.

After she replied no, he began telling her the truth. He told her when the addiction began, how it began, and how it has caused destruction in our marriage. He explained that pretty much anytime she has seen us fighting, it has been related to that.

The car went back to being silent. I sat there in awe, never expecting him to expose his secret to her. I was very proud of him. For the first time in our 16 years of marriage, he was taking responsibility for the one thing we just couldn't seem to fix.

Chapter Thirteen

DROPPING THE EXTRA WEIGHT

The hardest part about forgiveness is that it's not a one-time thing. Choosing to forgive someone who has broken your trust is a constant choice you have to make, sometimes hoping your emotions can catch up to the action. Triggers lurk around every corner, and intrusive thoughts begin to take your thoughts on a wild ride. I constantly had to remind myself that by choosing forgiveness, I would not be using past transgressions in arguments. When I was doubting or found myself worried, I would make the choice to trust. It was an uphill battle.

A few years ago, we went on vacation with another family to Destin, Florida. We really needed the vacation, left behind the real world for a week, and enjoyed the salty air. Zach had connected with the husband of this family on a hunting trip out west one year. While I had known the husband from our youth, it was the first time I had met his wife and kids. Their family mirrored our family. We both had two children, and their ages aligned. Our husbands got along and enjoyed the same topics and hobbies. That meant my friend for the week was the other wife.

The two of us went to the grocery store together to get food and snacks for the week. Before we left, she discovered that she had lost her wallet. We searched the trucks, the house we were staying in, and all the bags before we finally found it in the glove box of her truck. Now we were off to the grocery store.

As we walked around, she began grabbing things she liked, checking the prices to see which was cheaper. I was a little flustered because I needed a list of all the ingredients for each of the meals. We needed meals with ingredients or spices we could reuse later so there would be no waste. I wanted to know if there were days we planned to eat out and what snacks our kids shared interest in, so we only had to buy a few things rather than everyone's favorites. I tried to politely compromise on the simpler things and suggest alternatives when appropriate.

We returned to the house, unloaded the truck, took everything inside, and placed them on the counter. I tried to organize a little. After all, we would be living there for a week, and I needed some sort of order. When all the kids, husbands, and the other wife went out back to play in the pool, I went to my bedroom and began unpacking and organizing my belongings for the week.

As the week continued, I observed how this other woman engaged with her husband, her kids, and my family. She seemed so free, and it was captivating. She played with all the kids, got buried in sand holes, wore silly goggles, and at one point jumped in the pool with all her clothes on. I began to evaluate my life.

DROPPING THE EXTRA WEIGHT

When I was growing up, my mother always called me her flower child. I loved bright and wild colors. I effortlessly saw the best things in life. I was cheerful, social, and always happy. Where did that girl go? Who had I become? I missed that girl. Somewhere along the way of the Marine Corps, the hospital, becoming a mom, and arguing with my husband daily, I had no room for that girl. For the first time in probably 10 years, I realized I was no longer myself. I had become very serious in all the surviving I had been doing.

During the remaining days of our vacation, I made a goal to try to relax. I played when my kids asked, I rode a boogie board, and I let the dishes sit after dinner. From my experience, chores never disappear. I could tend to them after I played a little. I found it a challenge to play. I didn't always want to, but my kids were having such a great time with the other woman that I wanted to bring that same joy to them. I wanted to carry her same level of effortless energy. I wanted to experience my children the same way she was.

After another long day at the beach, the eight of us packed up and walked back to our rental. It was no surprise that the kids dropped everything in the driveway for the adults to rinse off and ran to the back yard to jump into the pool and cool off. The adults all knew that bellies would soon be hungry from a day in the sun, and we should start preparing dinner. We needed a few things for dinner, so the other wife and I took off for the local grocery store.

We returned to an empty house. Kids and husbands were still in the pool, awaiting our return, or maybe not. Maybe they were just continuing to enjoy what was left of their vacation. We walked out to the pool to let everyone know we had made it back.

The kids were doing flips into the pool, splashing and carrying on, and our husbands began splashing and taunting us to get in. Fully dressed, we squealed and begged them to knock it off. After much taunting, we decided to join them. I turned around to head inside and change into my swimsuit. I was about halfway to the door when I stopped. I turned around and ran toward the pool. As my feet left the ground and my body lunged for the pool, aiming for the spot directly in front of my husband, I grabbed my knees in my best efforts to do a cannon ball and give him a big splash.

It was an informal baptism. I came up from the water changed. I felt lighter and free from the burdens that had weighed me down for so long. It was fun. I was fun. I was playing with my husband for the first time in a very long time.

On our way home from that vacation, I took a photo of the four of us in the truck and posted it to Facebook. My mother-in-law commented on it, saying how we looked good and well-rested. For the first time, I actually felt well and rested with my life.

I didn't want this feeling to stop. I had reached the end yet again of my self-sufficiency. It is an ongoing battle. In our world, we are encouraged to be self-sufficient. That makes us strong, independent individuals. And while I believe it is sustainable for a while, it is not sustainable in the long term. Eventually, we will need rest and will come to the end of our own strength. I don't ever want to be self-sufficient. I want to always seek God for His wisdom and discernment, and I want my life to run on His never-ending strength and power. I want to rest in His presence and know that He will always take care of me just as He always has.

Somewhere along the way I heard this: "It's my job to trust you. It's your job to be trustworthy." I love this quote. I can't make someone be honest with me. I can, however, choose to do my part and believe someone when they say they are telling me the truth. Knowing that honesty is not always the case, I felt like I needed to add a little more for my own peace of mind. It's my job to trust you, and I will try. But ultimately, I trust God. I know He will reveal anything hidden.

I found more security in placing my trust in God. He had never let me down, and He has always kept His promises. I would trust God to continue to keep His promises. I found comfort in knowing that God redeems things that are stolen (Deut. 30:2–10). He is close to the brokenhearted. He sees my tears and hears my cries (Ps. 34:18), and He will rescue me from every evil attack (2 Tim. 4:18). My journey to trust would start with God front and center in my life.

Chapter Fourteen

FINDING ME AND FINDING PURPOSE

I began living my life each day knowing that I was not alone, that through every detail of my day I was seen, loved, and accompanied by the Holy Spirit. I trusted that God saw all my heartaches and that He would redeem the things in my life that felt like they had been stolen from me. God knew the two years I had spent living in a hospital. He knew my first pregnancy was away from family and friends, and less celebrated than ideal. God knew my first year of marriage was more trial than blessing. I had a choice, and I chose to no longer live as a victim to those things. I was going to live believing that those things, along with other past and future setbacks, would be returned to me and in better condition than I once experienced them.

I was 27 years old and in my final year of college when some coworkers and I decided to run a 5K. After weighing myself and seeing the scale one pound shy of 200, I had to do something. I could not fathom the scale tipping over to 200 pounds. Without hesitation, I agreed to join them in the 5K. As I set out to begin training, it became clear to me that this was going to be more difficult than I was expecting. Unable to run a full 60 seconds, I was determined to train all summer to run the full 3.1 miles without walking.

Three days a week I set out for my run and walk. Each week I found myself running longer and walking less. I was proud of the small victories I was accomplishing. In addition to running more, my clothes began fitting more loosely, and the numbers on the scale were decreasing at a steady pace. What I didn't expect was how much I was falling in love with my time out on the road. It was just me out there. No one could ask for a cup of milk, a snack, or help with anything. Nope. No one could interrupt me in this sacred time. Zach had to tend to his own needs and the kids' needs for roughly 30 minutes. While this was difficult at first, I quickly learned to embrace this time by listening to music, podcasts, or simply the steady blissfulness of my feet tapping on the asphalt.

What I had set out to do was accomplish a 5K with some friends, but what I ended up doing was finding myself. I fell in love with running. I loved having something just for me. I loved my time alone, and I loved that I was setting goals and accomplishing them on my own. Stress, weight, and symptoms of premenstrual dysphoric disorder (PMDD), something I had dealt with for the past 14 years, were all leaving me with every step I took. I was healing inside and out, and falling in love with myself at the same time.

That fall I completed my first 5K and haven't stopped running since. I went on to participate in countless 5Ks, 10Ks, half marathons, and a full marathon. I have learned through each of the training cycles that running is mostly mental and forces me to push past barriers I have created for myself. I've had to speak positively to myself and about myself. When I am alone out there running for a long period of time, I become my worst enemy or my biggest supporter, and which one I choose determines how the run goes. Either way, I have to get back home, so I might as well make friends with myself out there.

When I first began running, I hated the idea of running with friends. I was either too slow, which was the case most of the time, and I don't like holding people back, or I was faster and didn't want to slow down for others. I liked being alone and became very comfortable with that until one day while out on a run I crossed paths with another mom whose kids attended the same school as mine. We exchanged hellos and joined one another for the remainder of our run. Soon we were planning our runs together, and over time, we developed a unique bond. If you've ever been in a situation where you are physically exhausted, pushed past your comfort zone, and no longer caring about how you look or sound, you find yourself very willing to be vulnerable. These runs became gems of conversation where God was invited, secrets were shared, and judgment was not allowed. On these runs, we cried, laughed a lot, played in the rain and mud, and made some silly mistakes. When we finished each run, we came back much lighter and let our burdens go.

The running community is filled with supportive runners pushing and motivating one another regardless of your pace. There is a place for us all. I am a talker while I run, so I have met people from all over the world and enjoyed hearing where they come from, where they run, and whatever else they are willing to share. One thing I have come to realize is that whether running or sitting down for coffee, we have all walked through trials and have a story to tell. We have all faced things that have broken us, things we weren't sure we could get through, and things we didn't want to go through, and yet we made it to the other side.

For most of us, people can't see from the outside what we've been through, but when our scars are visible to the world, the curious world wants to know what happened. Zach and I get asked a lot if he served in the military or, more bluntly, "How did he lose his legs?" After answering them, we get a follow-up: "Oh, I am so sorry." That is when the real story begins. "Don't be sorry for us. It was a blessing we never would have asked for. We've grown, learned to love, learned to forgive, and learned that tomorrow is not promised."

We've been able to share our hurts, our setbacks, our accomplishments, and our journey through IVF and embryo adoption. I am far too stubborn to allow the enemy to own my life, and the pain we have walked through won't be in vain. I'll forever use it to glorify God, show how He changed our calloused and selfish hearts, how He gave us our babies, and how He loved us through the valleys and saved our lives and marriage.

I want to honor God by showing others the same compassion and comfort He has shown me (2 Cor. 1:3–4). I want all the awful things I have experienced to have purpose and not be in vain. I never want to forget that God always kept His promises, protected me, and saved me. I want my life to honor Him (Micah 6:4–8).

I still get caught up being discouraged when I cannot move mountains, when my help or input is too small, and when I want to offer something that makes a big difference. I have to remember that mountains are moved one small stone at a time. We can't all be preachers or missionaries, but we do all have a purpose.

That's when I am reminded that we are all part of one body. We each have different gifts and callings on our lives. Each one of us is important and valuable in completing the full body of Christ, His church (1 Cor. 12:12–31). I am best used in the area God has called me, and I cannot compare myself or my calling to someone else's. It took years for me to figure this out, years spent thinking I didn't have a calling on my life. But when I finally realized how God was using me in the lives of others, I was quickly encouraged and found that serving God felt natural and often effortless. He had already provided me with the tools I needed, and the ones I didn't have yet He provided when He knew I was ready.

God has given Zach and me a unique platform. We travel all over the United States and the world as Zach competes in marathons and paracycling events. We travel as a couple, a strong united team, as Zach sets out to accomplish his goal, the Paralympics. We've met some very amazing people and have also found ourselves in some unfavorable situations. As we navigate all the highs and lows, we strive to keep our eyes on Christ in all the good and the bad. People have complimented us on the way we carry ourselves, and when they do, we point to Christ. You see, through the eyes of the world we have the right to complain, to be saddened by our limitations and the things that have happened to us. But through Christ, we have let these things go and have seen His goodness through them. That is the charm that people see. That is Christ within us.

God had given us a story to share with the world. We never know when someone is watching us pray over a meal, see us extend grace in an undeserving situation, or be kind to a stranger or generous with the things we have. We don't always have to sign up for a mission trip, although that's a great thing to do. Our lives are a mission trip, and we never know who we are going to impact or lead to Christ simply by the everyday things we do and say.

Chapter Fifteen
PURPOSE BEHIND THE PAIN

I have spent far too much time and energy trying to navigate this life on my own. I suffered in silence when friends and family were willing to help, and I have tried to endure challenges in my own strength without seeking Christ. I was able to do it on my own for a while, but it eventually caught up with me. I needed God's help, and part of His help was giving me people to walk through the hard days with.

My life slowly began to fall into place when I was able to recognize God's presence in my life. He had been so faithful to me all along. My eyes and ears had been protected as a child by not seeing or hearing some of the things that were happening close to me. God used my parents to show me the importance of boundaries. Part of love is discipline and boundaries. I saw God's hand in Zach's life when he was spared from death and given a second chance at life. God has always been with us, working on our hearts.

I've seen God's gentle hand at work through the loneliness, anger, and disappointments I had set my eyes on. I wasn't just delivered from them; He showed me who He was through them, teaching me that I was not alone and could find rest in Him. God gave me mercy and asked me to do the same for others.

Tragedy, pain, rejection, and disappointments all revealed purpose and a greater plan for my life. My life isn't about me. My story isn't just mine.

> *Praise be to the God and Father of our Lord Jesus Christ, the Father of compassion and the God of all comfort, who comforts us in all our troubles, so that we can comfort those in any trouble with the comfort we ourselves receive from God. For just as we share abundantly in the sufferings of Christ, so also our comfort abounds through Christ. If we are distressed, it is for your comfort and salvation; if we are comforted, it is for your comfort, which produces in you patient endurance of the same sufferings we suffer.*
>
> —2 Cor. 1:3–6

I will continue to share my story with others in the hope that it will bring comfort, the same comfort I needed. I won each battle I faced, which taught me who God is. I will honor Christ with my life and share my story to pour into others the same hope and comfort I received. I will remind myself and them that God was, is, and will always be faithful.

For a very long time, I struggled with feeling robbed of the good things in life. I kept a running list. I was robbed of my early 20s, of my first pregnancy, of my first married years, of having a second child naturally. I felt robbed of being happy, and most of that I blamed on my husband. I felt like I had been a good person and didn't deserve the things that were happening to me. I longed for the next thing that would make me happy. I would be happy if my husband changed the things he was doing. I would be happy if I could have a second baby. I would be happy with a new home or a degree to get me out of my marriage. I got all those things eventually, but they didn't deliver the freedom or joy they seemed to promise.

    I exhausted all resources searching for this missing joy in my life, this freedom, until I broke down and cried out in an empty car. Jesus was right there all along, waiting so patiently for me to run into His open arms. I prayed for my life to change. I begged for happiness in whatever form God wanted me to receive it. I told God all about the wrongs that had been done to me, and then I was reminded of all the wrongs I, too, was committing. I had to ask for forgiveness for my own selfish heart. Then I had to turn my life over to Christ fully, no strings attached this time.

    Some things changed right away, And some things took years. Zach and I both had to break some old habits. We had to rebuild our communication and learn to listen when the other one spoke. And we had to do that without being defensive. It was hard. I turned my heart over to God each day, and I saw that my heart was changing quickly. The more I understood who God was, the more I knew who I was. The very things I had spent most of my life fearing, I discovered God had already provided what I needed to overcome.

    I was seen, heard, and loved and always would be. Anyone or anything cannot take away the joy God has given me. I know that my God loves me and never leaves me. I know that God has already conquered every situation I face.

My joy will no longer come from the people or things of the world that will leave me unsatisfied and wanting more. I will find my joy in Christ who loves abundantly and never changes. I will find happiness in the wonderful people and things of this world, allowing them to add to my life, but they will no longer control me. I will spend my life striving to honor Christ.

John 14:27 says, "Peace I leave with you; my peace I give you. I do not give to you as the world gives. Do not let your hearts be troubled and do not be afraid."

I learned to change the way I approached budding arguments with Zach. I became quick to be quiet rather than argue. I listened to him and walked away with all my anger and prayed, "God, you know what we both are trying to say. You know how we both feel. Help us communicate it." Most of the time, I came back to a diffused situation, and eventually we learned how to apologize. While I was busy trying to be a better woman and mother, I began to see that Zach was changing too.

While I don't want to speak for Zach, I will recall a moment when I was sitting beside him as he was doing an interview on a Zoom call. He was telling his story, from military to injured to athlete. I was in the same room, not seen by the cameras, just observing. Zach went on about some of his trials and the road that led him where he was at that time. Eventually, the interviewer asked Zach what his turning point was, the point where he turned his life around. Zach and I had never talked about this, and I had never thought to ask him. We had been doing really well for a couple years at that point, and I was interested in what he was about to say.

Tears ran down my face as I heard him tell the interviewer that he turned his life around when he thought he was losing his family. Mentally I could pinpoint the years he was referring to. I was struggling with staying. I had a plan to leave, and he must have felt that. When I surrendered my life to Christ and begged for happiness at any cost, letting go of arguments and praying more than I fought, it probably looked to him like I was distancing myself from him. I can't say for sure because I never had those conversations, but when I look back at the time that my entire focus was on Christ, it probably looked to Zach like I was pulling away from him.

God never ceases to amaze me. I love how He uses each of us in specific ways to lead others, even when we don't know we are doing it. I had no idea what Zach was thinking back then. I don't know that we ever had that conversation, but I do believe with all my heart that God had a plan to save our marriage and has a plan to use our marriage.

Chapter Sixteen

THE BATTLE IS ALREADY WON

As a little girl, I never fantasized about a life that told this story. I never expected to be a caregiver to my husband at the age of 21. I didn't expect that marriage would be so hard. I didn't anticipate infertility or embryo adoption. I quickly learned that my life and marriage were going to be a lot different than what I had role-played as a little girl. At 21, I found the harsh reality of life as a caregiver to an injured Marine. I was married and had a child but felt more like a single parent. I felt lost in a world that felt bigger than what I could carry, and I felt the pressure of everyone depending on me.

I felt lonely, and because I didn't share that with anyone, I became angry and eventually bitter and resentful toward my husband who I blamed for most of my anger. I hid it for as long as I could until it began to seep out of me.

Tomorrow came with troubles of its own. I pushed through for as long as I could, struggling until I couldn't take it anymore and finally leaned on God. I spent many years fighting every battle alone. I didn't confide in my family or my friends. I fought with my own strength until I couldn't do it, and I finally broke. It was the fear my mom had expressed years earlier when I tried to reassure her that I was fine.

What I learned was that God was there waiting patiently for me all along, and He was better at solving my problems than I ever would be. I had taken the hard road for a long time, trying to be the savior for myself and my family.

Surrendering my life to Christ doesn't promise a problem-free life. In fact, the Bible says the very opposite. What life with Christ does mean is that I don't have to face these battles alone. The overwhelming world and chaos that tries to take away my peace is not successful when I trust that God will care for me just like He always has. I can rest in the arms of a loving, kind, and gracious Father who wants my attention.

It was a humble pill to swallow when the Holy Spirit showed me that it was my heart that needed to change. I told God about all the things Zach was not doing right. I told God that my life would be easier if Zach would just follow Christ and lead his family to do the same. We would be better if Zach would just get it together. In the midst of all that prayer, my broken, hurt, bitter heart was guilty of its own transgressions.

I was failing Zach by holding him to expectations he was ill-equipped for at the time. He'd get there, but at that time I was only setting him up for failure. I had failed him in that way. I was failing in my own ways. I had thought I was more righteous than Zach. After all, I was the one praying and seeking Jesus. I was being active in our children's lives. I was going to school and work. I was the one making something of my life. I elevated myself to think I was living some sort of holy life and had the answers for the people around me.

Our marriage was suffering, and I believed it was all Zach's fault. I knew that if our marriage ended, it wasn't because of me. I did the best I could. I was kind for the most part. I certainly wasn't unfaithful on any level. I was the better parent for sure. Boy, oh boy, did my heart need a full makeover. I had to let go of everything, and when I was finally ready, it was easy to do. I was ready to be happy at any cost.

I let go of trying to control my husband and managing his every move. I let go of the expectations I had put on him. I let go of my hurt and pain and asked the Lord to take it all. I trusted that God saw every tear and knew how badly I hurt. I gave the Lord full control of my life. I had nothing left. I tried it all, and all of it failed. I did not care what I would walk through. I had no more to give and nothing to lose. I had peace that God would heal me.

Romans 5:1–11 tells us that we can boast in the hope of the glory of God. We can glory in our sufferings because they produce perseverance, which produces character, and character produces hope. God's love has been poured into our hearts through the Holy Spirit. I believe this fully. I believe that through these journeys I have walked through, I have seen Christ in my life in ways I never would have without the suffering. I have comfort in knowing that Christ died for me while I was still a sinner and that He didn't wait for me to be righteous first. He loved me in my brokenness and in my mess.

The more I leaned into God, the more I saw Him working in my life. He exposed sins effortlessly. I didn't have to search or catch Zach. Things that had been hidden in darkness were brought to light. I learned I could fully trust that God saw the things I couldn't and that He would take care of them, even the things I would never see. I could walk away from arguments and allow God to soften our hearts and speak to us in the silence.

It is evident to me that my marriage is protected by God. Together, Zach and I have been through a lot, and God has kept us. I believe God wants our marriage even more than we do, so I fully trust Him with my marriage. It's not just my marriage. He wants it all—my life, marriage, kids, friendships, jobs, hobbies, everything.

We fear the things we cannot control, the things that seem bigger than we are, but our God is so much bigger than anything we fear. We will walk through trials and experience pain and disappointment. We will know fear and worry, but we can have faith that God sees. He will walk us through the valleys and command the mountains to move and the seas to part. All we have to do is let go of our death grip on the situation, give God some room to work, trust that His way is better than ours, and know that He is for us.

I don't know what lies ahead of us or how our story ends. I do know that God loves me, sees me, and is for me.

> *For I am convinced that neither death nor life, neither angels nor demons, neither the present or the future, nor any powers, neither height nor depth, nor anything else in all creation, will be able to separate us from the love of God that is in Christ Jesus our Lord.*
> —Rom. 8:38–39

The battle is already won, and God holds the victory!

www.ingramcontent.com/pod-product-compliance
Lightning Source LLC
Chambersburg PA
CBHW070201100426
42743CB00013B/2998